The Legacy Blueprint

Maximize Potential

Volume One

Marvin St Macary

Stmacary Innovative Group, LLC

Preface

Leadership has never been about titles, positions, or platforms. At its core, leadership is influence—the ability to inspire, shape, and move people toward a vision greater than themselves. The challenge for many isn't whether they have influence, but whether they know how to maximize it.

This book was born out of two worlds I've lived in: the fast-paced, high-pressure culture of the entertainment industry and the deeply spiritual, people-centered world of ministry. On one side, I learned strategy, systems, and the art of execution. On the other, I discovered the necessity of humility, service, and spiritual grounding. Over time, I realized that effective leadership requires both: the wisdom to lead people well and the practical tools to move vision forward.

The Leadership Blueprint: Maximize Influence is not a collection of theories. It's a field guide. It's the lessons I've lived, the mistakes I've made, and the principles I've proven true in boardrooms, backrooms, and sanctuaries. My hope is that as you turn these pages, you'll find both clarity and courage—the clarity to see where your influence can expand, and the courage to lead with greater conviction.

This is not just about building successful organizations. It's about building healthy ones. Not just about achieving results, but about shaping people. Because leadership isn't only measured by what you accomplish—it's measured by who you impact along the way.

So I invite you to lean in. Mark up these pages. Wrestle with the ideas. Apply what resonates. Share it with your team. And most importantly, commit yourself to becoming the kind of leader whose influence outlives them.

If you maximize your influence, you don't just change the room you're in—you change the world around you.

Trusted with the Weight

Leadership Is Not About Power—It's About
Weight

Bishop James Nelson Jr. is one of my favorite preachers
and a great man of God who has profoundly impacted my life over
the past ten years. I'll never forget one moment when he visited the
Ramp Church and called me out to speak a Word of the Lord.

He prophesied blessings, open doors in business, harvest from
seeds I had sown, and great success. It was the kind of prophecy that
makes you want to shout or fall out on the spot. But before I could
rejoice, he ended with a statement that froze me in place:

"If you procrastinate in pursuing God's assignment over your life,
you will not only delay your blessings—you will hold up the blessings
of the people in the church."

I still fell out, but even as I lay on the floor, that statement echoed
in my spirit. Suddenly, I felt the weight of leadership in a way I never
had before. I didn't want to be the reason people missed their potential. I realized in that moment: leaders don't just carry vision—they
carry responsibility.

Leadership is not about position, title, or even power—it's about weight. It's the sobering reality that your choices don't just affect you; they affect the people who trust you, follow you, and look to you for guidance.

As a son of God, I want to live right because I love Him. But as a pastor, I also want to live right because I am responsible for people. When God places lives under your leadership—whether in a church, a business, or a family—He also places their outcomes within the reach of your decisions. That doesn't mean you control their every choice, but it does mean you are accountable for the culture you create, the example you set, and the standards you uphold.

Leadership isn't only about where you're going—it's about who you're taking with you, and how your decisions either lighten or weigh down the journey for those walking beside you.

The Ripple Effect of Leadership

A leader's decisions rarely remain private—they ripple.

• **In the family:** A father's neglect can shape how his children love, trust, and build their own homes. Conversely, a father's faithfulness creates security that strengthens generations.

• **In business:** One executive's unethical choice can collapse a company, costing thousands of jobs. But one leader's integrity can safeguard livelihoods for years.

• **In the church:** A pastor's failure can cause some to lose faith in God, not just in leadership. But a pastor's faithfulness can inspire people to endure storms they never thought they could survive.

Scripture gives us examples. Moses struck the rock, and an entire generation wandered. David's sin with Bathsheba led to death, division, and disqualification. Samson's indulgence with Delilah cost him his strength, his sight, and his influence.

Their private decisions had public consequences. That's the weight of leadership. It's not just about what you can carry—it's about what others might drop if you fall.

. . . .

Leadership Requires Restraint

Paul declared, *"If what I eat causes my brother or sister to fall into sin, I will never eat meat again, so that I will not cause them to fall"* (1 Corinthians 8:13, NIV).

That is the voice of a leader—someone who understands that love limits liberty. A leader says, *"I could, but I won't—because they're watching."*

• A leader doesn't post everything online—not because it's sinful, but because it could confuse the people following them.

• A leader doesn't go everywhere their peers go—not because they feel superior, but because their presence carries influence.

• A leader doesn't say everything they feel in anger—not because the emotions aren't real, but because they know the cost of careless words.

Leadership requires restraint. You willingly lay down some freedoms—not because God doesn't love you, but because others are drawing strength from your life. Every choice is a seed, and every seed you plant will eventually bear fruit in the people who follow your example.

The Burden That Builds You

The weight of leadership is not meant to crush you—it is meant to keep you sober, humble, and dependent on God. It reminds us that charisma may attract a crowd, but character keeps people covered.

This is why Jesus said, *"To whom much is given, much is required."* It's why Paul urged Timothy: *"Watch your life and your doctrine closely. Persevere in them, because if you do, you will save both yourself and your hearers"* (1 Timothy 4:16, NIV).

• My integrity affects their stability.

• My consecration protects their covering.

• My discipline determines how far we go together.

Leadership is not about perfection—it is about responsibility. If

God has called you to lead, He has also called you to walk with wisdom, humility, and honor. Not only for your sake, but for theirs.

Because people may never remember every sermon you preached, every meeting you led, or every decision you made—but they will never forget how your choices shaped their lives.

One careless moment can fracture trust. But a consistent life of integrity can build a legacy that outlives you.

The Entry Level of Elevation

Serve Your Way In

I was in Los Angeles, working for the legendary music video director Hype Williams, when he asked me to meet him at a gym called Sports Club L.A.

This wasn't your average gym. When I walked in, it felt more like a five-star resort than a place to sweat. The lighting was perfect. The air was scented. Inside, there was a sushi bar, a massage area, a salon, valet parking, a full-size basketball court, and a gorgeous pool deck.

As I stood there, taking it all in, the actor Mark Wahlberg walked past. Supermodels floated by like it was a scene out of a movie. And in that moment, I thought to myself: *I need to be here.*

Not because I wanted to work out—but because I wanted to be around that level of excellence and energy. So I went to the front desk and asked about a membership. That's when reality hit.

The registration fee alone was more than my rent. The monthly dues? Laughable. I couldn't afford it.

But instead of walking away discouraged, I asked myself: *What's the next best move?* So I applied for a job. If I couldn't pay my way in, I'd serve my way in.

. . .

Excuses or Ingenuity

Every leader faces moments where the door they want to walk through feels locked. Sometimes it's lack of money, status, experience, or opportunity. It's easy to stop at the barrier and call it final.

But true leaders don't see closed doors as denial. They see them as an invitation to get creative. As Proverbs reminds us, *"Wise people think before they act"* (Proverbs 13:16, NLT).

Leadership isn't just about vision—it's about resourcefulness. It's finding a way forward when the obvious path isn't available. You may not have the funds, credentials, or connections yet—but what can you offer? Your service. Your time. Your attitude. Your hustle.

That gym taught me a principle I've carried throughout my life: Access doesn't always come by paying your way in. Sometimes you serve your way in.

Service Opened the Real Door

Once I got in the room—serving instead of spectating—I discovered something even more valuable than luxury amenities. I made connections with fashion moguls, entertainment lawyers, and record executives.

I didn't meet them at a networking event. I met them folding towels. I met them while showing up consistently with excellence.

They noticed my demeanor, my work ethic, my curiosity. I was no longer just an observer—I became a trusted presence. That's what serving does: it earns you access, trust, and proximity. It doesn't just get you in the room—it helps you belong there.

Jesus Taught the Same Thing

Jesus said, *"The greatest among you must be your servant"* (Matthew 23:11, NIV). He didn't just preach it—He lived it.

He served at tables before He was seated at the right hand of the Father. He washed feet before He walked on water. He served His way into influence. That's not just theology—it's strategy.

Some of the best access you'll ever gain won't come through money or position. It will come through humble service. And once you're in the room—serving, observing, learning—you begin absorbing wisdom and favor you couldn't have bought with a credit card.

What Happens When You Serve Your Way In

1 You Gain Proximity to Greatness

You don't just read about high-level thinkers—you work beside them. You see what excellence looks like up close.

2 You Get an Insider's Education

You learn the habits, language, and values of those operating on the next level. You stop dreaming abstractly and start preparing strategically.

3 You Build Relational Equity

Service earns trust. Trust opens doors. And those doors are often more permanent than the ones money can unlock.

4 You Grow in Humility and Hunger

You don't just want access—you value it. You've earned your seat, and that makes you show up differently.

What Room Do You Need to Enter?

Maybe you're trying to break into ministry leadership, entrepreneurship, or a new industry. And maybe the front door feels locked.

You might not be able to join right away—but can you help?

- Can you volunteer?
- Can you intern?
- Can you serve behind the scenes?
- Can you show up early, stay late, and become indispensable?

The world is full of people waiting for someone to open a door for them. But leaders learn to enter through the side gate, the back door, or even the service entrance—if that's what it takes. Because once you're inside, what you gain is priceless.

Lead Like a Doorkeeper

There's a verse in Psalms that captures the attitude perfectly: *"I'd rather be a doorkeeper in the house of my God than dwell in the tents of the wicked"* (Psalm 84:10, NIV).

Sometimes the lowest position puts you in the best location. I didn't get into that gym by flexing. I got in by folding towels and checking IDs. But what I learned while serving there shaped how I carry myself to this day.

So wherever you're trying to go—don't give up because the path isn't paved. Lead with humility. Serve with excellence. Be willing to work your way in.

Because leaders don't wait for access.

They create it.

Don't Be the Narcissistic Leader

Leadership Is Not a Spotlight—It's a Stewardship

Years ago, I attended an event where a well-known leader walked into the room. Before they said a word, the cameras were already on, the crowd stood to cheer, and the atmosphere felt electric. But as the night went on, I realized something sobering: all the energy was centered on him. Every story, every instruction, every moment somehow circled back to their accomplishments, their greatness, their image.

People left impressed—but not empowered. Inspired—but not equipped. The spotlight was bright, but it never moved beyond one person.

That night I learned a principle I've carried ever since: leadership isn't about being the star of the show—it's about stewarding the stage for others. If the mission dies when the spotlight moves, it wasn't leadership at all—it was performance.

One of the greatest pitfalls a leader can fall into is making leadership about themselves. When the mission begins revolving around your name, your image, your platform, or your applause, you've stopped leading and started performing.

Narcissistic leadership may build a crowd, but it will never build a community.

What Narcissistic Leadership Looks Like

We've all seen it. Leaders who:

- Need to be the smartest person in every room.
- Manipulate loyalty and confuse fear for respect.
- Correct everyone else but never reflect on themselves.
- Crush people under the weight of their own insecurities.

It's like the insecure coach who benches the most talented player so no one outshines him. Or the boss who takes credit for the team's hard work but vanishes when mistakes are made. Or the pastor who preaches humility on Sunday but refuses correction on Monday.

Narcissistic leaders treat people like stage props—useful only as long as they make them look good.

Charisma vs. Character

Charisma might attract people, but character keeps them. And narcissistic leaders often rely on charisma without cultivating character.

- They confuse being served with serving.
- They demand loyalty but never offer covering.
- They treat people as tools, not treasures.

That's why some leaders can pack auditoriums but can't build trust in a staff meeting. Their brand might be big, but their relationships are broken.

The Alternative: Servant Leadership

Healthy leadership flips the script. It's not about how many people serve you—it's about how faithfully you serve them.

In the entertainment industry, I watched talented leaders sabotage their teams because they were more obsessed with the mirror than the mission. Their focus was on their brand, their narrative, their elevation.

But real leaders don't need a stage to shine—they create platforms for others to stand on.

Jesus, the greatest leader the world has ever known, modeled this. He washed feet. He led with humility. He corrected with grace. He called out greatness in others rather than constantly rehearsing their flaws. His leadership didn't crave attention—it created transformation.

• When the disciples argued about who was the greatest, Jesus reminded them: *"The greatest among you will be your servant"* (Matthew 23:11, NIV).

• When Peter failed Him, Jesus restored him instead of replacing him.

• When others saw outcasts, Jesus saw sons and daughters.

Signs You Might Be Sliding Into Narcissism

Here are a few warning lights on the leadership dashboard:

• You talk more than you listen.

• You surround yourself with people who only agree with you.

• You react to feedback as if it's a personal attack.

• You use your position to control rather than empower.

• You view other people's success as a threat instead of a win.

If any of those sting, good. Awareness is where healing begins.

Why This Matters

Leadership isn't about perfection—it's about accountability. And when you heal from the need to be celebrated, you free yourself to be impactful.

- You don't have to prove your worth.
- You don't have to compete with your team.
- You don't have to chase the spotlight to be effective.

Your value doesn't come from being the hero—it comes from helping others rise.

The Legacy of Healthy Leadership

Great leaders don't point to themselves. They point to the mission. They empower others. They build legacies, not fan clubs.

History shows us the difference:

- **Narcissistic Leaders**: Saul lost his kingdom because he cared more about his image than God's instruction. Diotrephes in 3 John loved to be "first" and ended up dividing the church.
- **Healthy Leaders**: Moses poured into Joshua. Elijah released a double portion to Elisha. Paul raised up Timothy and Titus. Jesus entrusted the future of the church to ordinary disciples.

The contrast is clear: narcissists hoard influence. Servants multiply it.

The Call

If you're in leadership—whether in church, business, or your home—do the inner work. Lay down your ego. Starve the need for applause.

Because the greatest leaders aren't the ones with the loudest voices. They're the ones who make others feel seen, heard, and empowered.

So lead with love. Lead with humility. Lead with purpose.

But whatever you do... don't become the narcissistic leader.

The Wisdom of Silence

Shut Up Sometimes

"Even fools are thought wise when they keep silent; with their mouths shut, they seem intelligent." (Proverbs 17:28, NLT)

There's a kind of wisdom that doesn't show up in what you say—it shows up in what you choose not to say. Every young leader must learn the balance between confidence and humility, between having a voice and knowing when to hold it.

The Day I Spoke Too Soon

While interning at Bad Boy Entertainment, I was surrounded by legends—industry giants whose names carried weight. My role was simple: serve, support, observe, and learn. That's it.

I was invited into rooms, but not into conversations. And I understood that—until one day, my enthusiasm got the best of me.

I had to deliver a document to my boss, who happened to be in conversation with none other than Mase—the platinum-selling rapper himself. They were reviewing SoundScan numbers, the industry's weekly report on album sales.

As I handed her the folder, Mase casually asked:

"Do you think 330,000 first-week record sales is a good number?"

Before my boss could respond, I—just a hungry intern with a strong opinion—blurted out:

"Oh no. DMX sold over 640,000 in his first week. Anything less than that is trash."

The room froze. Mase looked at me and calmly replied:

"My album sold 330,000 copies."

Embarrassment hit me like a tidal wave. I wanted to melt into the floor. Without a word, I turned around and walked out as fast as I could.

That moment seared a truth into me I never forgot: Not every room is asking for your opinion. Sometimes the most powerful thing you can say is nothing at all.

Your Job Is to Learn, Not Lead—Yet

When you're young, gifted, and eager to prove yourself, silence can feel like invisibility. But it's not. Silence is preparation. Silence is strategy. Silence gives you space to observe, absorb, and gain wisdom that premature words might cost you.

"You don't learn by dominating the room. You learn by listening in it."

That moment at Bad Boy wasn't about record sales—it was about knowing my role and respecting the weight of experience around me. I wasn't there to flex knowledge. I was there to gain it.

"In the multitude of words sin is not lacking, but he who restrains his lips is wise." (Proverbs 10:19, NKJV)

Don't Mistake Access for Authority

Being in the room doesn't mean you've earned the mic. Proximity to greatness is a privilege—but that privilege can be lost through a lack of humility.

I had been trusted with access, but I hadn't yet earned influence. My voice was premature. And it taught me a crucial truth:

If you speak too soon, you might be heard. But if you wait for wisdom, you'll be remembered.

The Best Leaders Were Once Great Listeners

• Jesus didn't launch His ministry until He spent 30 years in silence, study, and surrender.

• David didn't rule as king the moment he was anointed—he served in the fields, listening and learning before leading on the throne.

• Solomon asked for wisdom before he ever asked for wealth.

You don't lose influence by being quiet. You gain credibility by discerning when your voice is needed.

"Everyone should be quick to listen, slow to speak." (James 1:19, NIV)

Modern Examples of Premature Voices

• **Workplace**: An intern correcting the CEO in a board meeting instead of soaking in decades of experience.

• **Ministry**: A new preacher rewriting theology on Instagram before learning the basics of pastoral care.

• **Family**: A teenager lecturing their parents about marriage when they haven't even paid a light bill.

Silence doesn't diminish you—it disciplines you.

Always Remember

• **Honor the Room** – Sometimes your presence is enough.

• **Listen to Learn, Not to Respond** – Every conversation is a classroom.

• **Let Humility Lead You** – You don't have to prove you're smart; your fruit will speak for you.

• **Timing Is Everything** – The right word at the wrong time is still the wrong word.

The Monkey Was in Charge

Leadership Rarely Goes According to Plan
You can have the vision mapped out, the team in place, and the goal clearly defined—but sooner or later, something will go left. And when it does, real leaders don't panic... they pivot.

One of the most memorable projects I ever worked on was the music video for Robin Thicke's *"Wanna Love You Girl"* featuring Pharrell Williams. We shot it in Punta Cana, Dominican Republic—a dream location. Clear waters. White sand. Palm trees swaying in the breeze. On the surface, it looked like paradise. And for a while, it was.

We had a small but talented crew—just seven or eight of us. I stepped into the role of producer, taking on more responsibility than I ever had on a set. But I was ready. Robin was a joy to work with, his then-wife Paula Patton brought grace and warmth, and his manager Miguel Melendez was as cool as they come. We worked hard all day, ate lobster at night, and let loose afterward. It felt like one of those rare moments where work, life, and creativity collided in perfect rhythm.

And to top it off—I even met someone special. One of the talent on set would later become my girlfriend for a couple of years. So yes, the vibes were high... until the monkey took over.

And That's When the Monkey Took Over

We had hired a local producer to manage logistics. Now, I've worked with some unique personalities—but this woman took eccentric to another level. She walked around set with a pet monkey. Not only did she treat him like a human—she acted like he was in charge. She'd have full conversations with him, asking his thoughts on production schedules, weather conditions, you name it.

And honestly? The more we watched her, the more we joked that maybe the monkey really was running things. Because it quickly became clear: she had nothing prepared. No permits. No backup plans. No sense of order. Just vibes, chaos, and her monkey.

It got so bad that Hype Williams, the director, pulled me aside and said:

"I don't trust her with the footage. I need you to take the daily reels and fly them back to Miami every night, drop them off at the film processing house, and then fly back to set in the morning."

I nodded, but inside I was thinking: *You've got to be kidding me.*

To get to the airport, I had to take a one-hour flight on a tiny four-seater plane to Santo Domingo. From there, I'd board a commercial flight to Miami, deliver the footage, and then do it all over again—every night until the shoot wrapped.

But here's the thing: we had promised the client a video. And when a promise is made, a leader's job is to do whatever it takes to make sure the vision is fulfilled.

So even though I hated the task, I agreed.

Flying Through the Storm

The first night, I climbed into that small plane with the reels, two pilots, and a bodyguard assigned to protect me. Mid-air, a brutal storm hit. The turbulence was violent. The plane shook uncontrollably. The pilots spoke rapidly in Spanish, clearly alarmed.

I turned to my bodyguard and asked, "What are they saying?"

He hesitated, then finally answered: *"They said… they don't think we're going to make it."*

Now, I wasn't saved at the time—but I knew exactly who to call on. *"Jesus!"* I whispered.

By the grace of God, we landed safely. But I was done. There was no way I was getting back on another small plane. I demanded we drive the four hours back to set instead. I didn't care how long it took —I just needed pavement under my feet again.

When I finally returned, I braced myself for Hype's frustration. Technically, I had failed the assignment. But when he saw me, he burst out laughing.

"I heard what happened," he said. *"I'm just glad you were willing to try. You were flexible. That's what matters."*

The Lesson That Stayed With Me

That moment taught me a lesson I've carried ever since: Sometimes leadership means switching roles, embracing the uncomfortable, and stepping outside your title to protect the bigger picture.

One day you're the producer. The next, you're the courier. The next, you're holding on for dear life in a storm over the Caribbean.

But the goal remains the same: Honor the assignment. Finish the job. Deliver the vision.

"Whatever you do, work at it with all your heart, as working for the Lord, not for human masters." (Colossians 3:23, NIV)

Looking back, I realize that even though I didn't yet have a relationship with God, He was already covering me—protecting me, preserving me. And now, as a believer and a leader in ministry, I understand the principle even more clearly:

• There's no room for ego when you're on assignment.

• God isn't impressed by titles—He's looking for obedience.

• Sometimes He'll ask you to fly through storms. Other times He'll ask you to carry the weight no one else wants to.

The reward isn't just in completing the task—it's in the posture of your heart. When you serve with excellence, flexibility, and faithfulness, even in uncomfortable situations, heaven takes notice.

So yes—the monkey might be in charge. The set might fall apart. The storm may come.

But a leader pivots. A leader stays flexible. A leader gets the job done.

And the one who endures with a willing heart? That's the one God can trust with the next assignment.

You Can't Force Chemistry

You Can't Cheat the Process

In leadership, there's always a temptation to build fast. We see opportunity, feel the pressure, and scramble to put something together that looks like it works—even if it's duct-taped by potential.

But here's what I learned the hard way: You can't force chemistry. You have to build it.

The Setup: Bad Boy Dreams and Big Plans

In my early days interning at Bad Boy Entertainment, I was hungry. I wasn't trying to coast—I was trying to climb.

One day, I met a guy who worked in one of the studios. He was well-connected and told me something that lit a fire under me:

"Timbaland is looking for a female version of Jodeci."

That was it. My shot.

We came up with a plan:

• He would produce the track and write the lyrics.

• I would find the group.

There was just one problem: I didn't know a group. But I did know gifted individuals.

At the time, I was in college, and our performing arts program was overflowing with talent. So, like any eager leader faced with opportunity, I did what seemed smart—I created a group out of four women who had never worked together.

The Makeshift Group

Individually, they were incredible:

• One was a powerful gospel singer who led worship at her church.

• Another had a Broadway-style voice with acting chops to match.

• One was an edgy Latina with hip-hop flair and confidence.

• The last was pure Neo Soul—Erykah Badu vibes all the way.

They all said yes. They'd seen each other around campus but weren't friends. Still, they agreed to try.

We had three days to rehearse. They worked hard, showed up, and by the third day it looked like maybe, just maybe, we had something.

The Audition

The studio was on the west side of 34th Street in Manhattan. We sat in the lounge, nerves tight, waiting for our turn. A tall gentleman stepped out and said he'd hear the group first. If he liked what he heard, he'd bring them in to sing for Timbaland.

They performed the song. Then he asked each of them to sing individually. No smile. No nod. Just stone-faced listening.

Finally, he asked:

"How long have you all been a group?"

One of the women quickly replied:

"A couple years."

He nodded, paused, and said:

"Well, keep practicing and come back in six months."

Before we could leave, one girl blurted:

"Would you consider me as a solo artist?"

His response was blunt:

"Not at this time."

We started walking out, deflated. Then he called us back.

"You two—stay behind."

Once the girls were gone, he looked us dead in the face and said:

"Why'd y'all waste my time? Those girls just met each other two days ago. That wasn't a group. You can't force chemistry. It has to be built."

That was the polite version.

Forced Doesn't Flow

That moment hit me like a gut punch.

What I thought was innovation was really improvisation. It had potential—but it didn't have authenticity.

The vocals weren't the problem. The problem was connection. There was no shared story. No synergy. No unity. Just four solo acts trying to perform as a group.

And here's the leadership principle: Talent doesn't equal team.

You Can't Microwave Unity

Whether it's a singing group, a business team, a church staff, or a leadership circle—chemistry is a process.

You have to:

- Spend time together.
- Learn each other's rhythms.
- Build trust.
- Work through tension.

• Discover how one person's strength complements another's weakness.

There's no shortcut for real connection. The most powerful teams don't just sound good—they move in harmony. They don't just rehearse together—they think together. That's the difference between performing together and operating as one.

Unity Requires Time

Jesus didn't throw the disciples into ministry on day one. He walked with them. Taught them. Corrected them.

He allowed room for disagreement and growth. Even Peter and John—so different in personality—became powerful together, but only after time in the trenches.

"How good and pleasant it is when God's people live together in unity." (Psalm 133:1, NIV)

Unity isn't sameness. It's alignment. And alignment comes from investment—time, trust, and truth.

Don't Build on Potential Alone

In leadership, the pressure to produce can push you to shortcut the process. But God's best is never rushed.

You don't just need people who can perform—you need people who can carry the weight with you.

Don't build fast—build real.

Don't just put people together—bring them together.

Because if it's not built right, it may look good for a moment...

But it will collapse under pressure.

Three Plays Ahead

Great Leaders Don't Just React—They Anticipate

One of the most underrated qualities in leadership is strategic foresight—the ability to see beyond the present moment and prepare for what isn't visible yet. It's what separates managers from visionaries.

It's not mystical. It's not guessing the future. It's the discipline of asking: *What's next? What's coming? And how can we prepare before the storm hits or the window closes?*

A Moment of Vision

I remember sitting in a meeting in Bishop S.Y. Younger's office with a few of our leaders. He began to share a fresh idea—something he felt impressed to do, even though things were going well.

He said: *"I think we need to develop an online church."*

Now, we were already live-streaming services on social media. But this was different. He envisioned a digital extension of our community—not just content, but connection:

- A pastor dedicated to online members
- Systems for follow-up and engagement
- Tools to build relationships beyond the building

At first, it sounded like something we'd grow into over time. But within a week, COVID-19 shut the world down.

Mass gatherings were banned. In-person church was suspended. Ministries everywhere scrambled to figure out what to do next. But thanks to that meeting—and more importantly, Bishop Younger's foresight—we were already in motion.

We didn't just survive that season—we served, we grew, and we stayed connected to our church family and beyond. Our teams adapted. Every Sunday we streamed worship, the Word, and encouragement to people around the world. And while many ministries faced financial collapse, we remained spiritually and financially stable.

All because one leader had the ability—and the discipline—to see past today.

Strategic Thinking Is a Leadership Muscle

Strategic foresight isn't about having random ideas—it's about the discipline to pause, plan, and prepare.

Bishop Younger didn't just think, *"That's interesting."* He sat with the idea. Brought it to the table. Involved his team. Put it into motion.

That's what strategic leadership looks like. It's not just creativity —it's conscious preparation. It's asking:

- What could change the way we serve?
- What risks are we not seeing?
- What opportunities should we seize before others do?
- If this fails tomorrow, are we ready?

Biblical Foresight: Joseph in Egypt

In Genesis 41, Joseph interpreted Pharaoh's dream of a coming famine. But he didn't stop at interpretation—he offered a plan: *"Let Pharaoh appoint commissioners... to collect a fifth of the harvest during the seven years of abundance."*

His foresight saved not only Egypt but nations beyond it.

Imagine if Joseph had waited until the famine hit before planning. That's the difference between reactive and strategic leadership: one waits for impact, the other builds the ark before it rains.

The Marks of a Strategic Leader

1 They Think Long-Term

They don't just ask what's best this week—they ask what's best for the next five years.

2 They Look for Weak Spots Before Crisis Hits

They identify areas of vulnerability before they become public failures.

3 They Plan for Both Possibility and Pressure

They build capacity for growth and contingency for crisis.

4 They Take Action on Insight

Ideas without execution are just daydreams. Real leaders strategize, not just talk.

The Call to Anticipate

God may give you a glimpse. A thought. A burden. Don't brush it off. Don't just be spiritual—be strategic.

Sit down. Write it out. Call your team. Build it.

Because the future belongs to those who prepare for what others ignore. You don't have to be a prophet to plan ahead. But if you're a leader, you must learn to look past the now and build what's next.

The Power of Rest and it's Ripple Effect

Rest Is Not a Luxury—It's a Leadership Responsibility

During my sophomore year at Fordham University, I was on what felt like an unstoppable mission. I was taking 20 credits, working part-time at the school library, juggling what felt like a full-time internship at Bad Boy Entertainment, and rehearsing for a stage production. Oh—and I was still clubbing hard every weekend.

Hustle was my language. Drive was my identity. I believed success meant always being in motion. Rest, in my mind, was for the weak. From the outside, it looked promising—my schedule was full, opportunities were opening, momentum was building. But inside, I was running on fumes—and I didn't even realize it.

The Dress Rehearsal Breakdown

After weeks of practice, we had our final dress rehearsal—open to an audience. I walked confidently on stage, ready to deliver. Then it happened.

Blank. My mind froze. My lines vanished. The cast tried to improvise, but the rhythm collapsed. I wasn't just off—I was absent.

Afterward, the director pulled me aside: *"Go home. Study your lines. We need you to show up tomorrow."*

I nodded, but instead of studying—I went home and slept. And then I slept some more.

The next night, rested and sharp, I nailed the role. The show flowed effortlessly, the cast came alive, and the audience responded.

That moment taught me leadership lessons I'll never forget.

Rest Is Not the Enemy of Progress

I had bought into the lie that constant motion equals success. But that rehearsal showed me: Rest is not the enemy of progress—it's the fuel of it.

Even Jesus, with the weight of the world on His shoulders, practiced intentional rest: *"Jesus often withdrew to lonely places and prayed."* He didn't rest because He was weak. He rested because He was wise.

If the Son of God needed rest, how much more do we?

Rest isn't laziness—it's obedience. It's trust. It's saying, *"God, I don't have to burn out to prove my worth. You called me, and You'll sustain me."*

We are not machines. We are vessels. And vessels must be filled. An empty vessel can't pour. A drained leader can't lead.

When a Leader Is Out of Alignment, Everyone Feels It

That night, my entire cast paid for my imbalance. That's the ripple effect of leadership: your private discipline—or lack of it—always has public consequences.

When a leader is tired, distracted, or unprepared, it trickles down. It affects morale, performance, and trust.

Jeremiah 10:21 says, *"The shepherds are senseless and do not inquire of the Lord; so they do not prosper, and all their flock is scattered."*

When leaders disconnect, people scatter. And this doesn't just apply to the stage—it happens in pulpits, boardrooms, classrooms, and homes. When you're running on fumes, everyone else feels the weight you've dropped.

Sabbath Is Sacred

God didn't suggest rest—He commanded it: *"Remember the Sabbath day by keeping it holy... On it you shall not do any work."* (Exodus 20:8–10, NIV)

Rest is worship. It's not just sleep—it's alignment. It's re-centering your soul and honoring the God who sustains you.

Burnout isn't a badge of honor—it's neglect. You can't pour oil if your flask is empty. And if leaders don't manage their energy, they will sabotage their assignment.

What I Learned

That week, I thought I needed more work. What I really needed was rest.

The enemy loves exhausted leaders because tired leaders are more reactive, more irritable, less discerning, and more vulnerable to distraction. But rested leaders? They see clearly, hear God distinctly, and lead with strength.

"Come to me, all you who are weary and burdened, and I will give you rest." (Matthew 11:28, KJV)

Rest is God's gift to leaders. Not to stop working—but so we can work from clarity, peace, and strength.

What I Know Now

• Rest isn't selfish—it's stewardship.

• When I don't take care of myself, I become a burden to others.

• As a leader, my health—mental, emotional, spiritual—affects the whole house.

• And sometimes, the most spiritual thing you can do is take a nap.

Now I don't just hustle—I plan for pauses. Because purpose is too important to be led by someone running on empty.

Leading From Rest, Not Empty

Leadership is demanding. You carry burdens, cast vision, resolve conflicts, and pour into others. But you can't pour if you're empty. And it's unfair to those you lead to only give them your leftovers.

Your team, your family, your ministry—they deserve the best of you, not what's left of you. If you model nonstop busyness, your people will too. And eventually, everyone burns out.

Rest is not weakness—it's wisdom. Jesus withdrew, paused, and prayed. If the One who carried the world made space to rest, so must we.

When you lead from rest:

• You hear more clearly.

• You respond with grace.

• You carry joy instead of just obligation.

Rest protects discernment. Rest restores creativity. Rest renews perspective.

So leader—take the rest. Your body needs it. Your family needs it. Your vision needs it. And your team deserves it.

Don't lead from empty. Lead from overflow.

Molders of Consensus

A **Genuine Leader Molds Consensus**

"A genuine leader is not a searcher for consensus but a molder of consensus." — Dr. Martin Luther King Jr.

Leadership is not about waiting to see what the crowd agrees on. It's about discerning what God has revealed and guiding people toward it.

In a culture obsessed with polling, popularity, and people-pleasing, genuine leaders must remember: we are not called to chase consensus, but to shape it. Great leaders listen, but they don't bow. They discern, but they don't dilute.

Consensus is not the starting point of leadership—it's often the result of it.

Consensus Is Comfortable, But Conviction Is Costly

Too many leaders fall into the trap of waiting for everyone to be on the same page before they move. They delay vision, avoid confrontation, and water down truth in the name of "unity."

But the goal of leadership isn't agreement—it's alignment.

Leaders are not thermometers, reflecting the temperature of the room. They are thermostats—they set the climate.

And real leadership costs.

• Jesus didn't poll the disciples before heading to Jerusalem.

• Moses didn't take a vote before confronting Pharaoh.

• Nehemiah didn't gather a focus group before rebuilding the wall.

They weren't reckless—but they weren't ruled by popular opinion either.

Vision Is Often Lonely at First

The path of a visionary leader is often misunderstood—especially in the beginning.

• Noah looked foolish building an ark before the rain.

• Abraham left everything without a map.

• Joseph's dreams provoked his brothers' hatred.

• Jesus preached a Kingdom that had not yet been seen.

What they shared wasn't universal agreement—it was divine conviction. They didn't need everyone to believe at first. They just needed enough conviction to begin.

Conviction must precede consensus.

Shaping Consensus Takes Strategy and Spirit

True leaders don't wait for consensus—but they don't ignore it either. Molding consensus requires both strategy and Spirit:

• **Clear Communication** – People follow clarity, not confusion.

• **Consistent Character** – People trust leaders whose lives echo their words.

• **Compassionate Conviction** – It's not just about being right, but about leading righteously.

Great leaders take what God gives them in the secret place and communicate it with enough vision, integrity, and humility that people begin to see it too.

Don't Be Afraid to Lead Before They Understand

If you wait for everyone to "get it" before you obey, you'll never move.

Sometimes the hardest part of leadership is pressing forward when those you love don't yet see what you see.

Jesus said to Peter in John 13:7: *"You do not realize now what I am doing, but later you will understand."*

That's leadership—doing what's necessary now, so others can understand later.

Leading in Ministry: Shepherds, Not Surveyors

In spiritual leadership—especially in the Church—this principle is even more critical.

We are not called to run ministries like politicians or entertainers.

We are shepherds, not surveyors.

Yes, we serve the people.

Yes, we listen.

Yes, we seek counsel.

But ultimately—we answer to God.

Kingdom leaders don't just manage momentum. They steward vision.

Practical Wisdom: How to Mold Consensus Without Manipulating People

• **Cast the vision in layers** – Some need to hear it more than once before it clicks.

• **Use testimonies and fruit** – People follow results more than rhetoric.

• **Build coalitions, not cliques** – Empower those who see the vision to echo it.

• **Model what you preach** – Your lifestyle gives your words authority.

• **Celebrate small wins** – Progress encourages participation.

Consensus doesn't happen instantly—but a consistent, Spirit-led leader can shape it over time.

Lead With Your Ear to Heaven, Not the Crowd

If you spend your life searching for consensus, you'll become a slave to the crowd. But if you commit your heart to molding it, you'll become a servant of purpose.

The crowd didn't crown David—God did.

The crowd didn't part the Red Sea—Moses' obedience did.

The crowd didn't save the world—Jesus did, by walking alone.

So stop waiting for everyone to be ready. Be the leader who makes them ready.

True leadership doesn't begin with applause—it begins with obedience.

And when you lead with conviction, consensus will eventually follow.

Code Switch

Leadership, Code-Switching, and the Power of Adaptability

There's a common joke in the Black community:

"We all know what voice to use with our friends... and what voice to use at work."

It's funny because it's true.

There's the *"what up fam"* voice, and there's the *"Hi, this is Marvin speaking"* voice.

That's called code-switching—the ability to adjust your tone, vocabulary, and presentation to fit your environment. But when you mature as a leader, you realize it's deeper than just sounding different. It's about reading the room, shifting with wisdom, and showing up authentically without compromising your assignment.

I Grew Up in a Cultural Mosaic

I grew up in New York City—a place where the world meets on one subway line.

The neighborhood I called home was Caribbean central. My

apartment building was filled with Haitians, Trinidadians, Jamaicans —and on any given Saturday, you could smell jerk chicken, hear zouk music, and see grandmothers shouting from balconies like prophets.

My high school? A whole different world.

I attended Xavier High School, a Jesuit institution that drew some of the brightest minds across the city. It was predominantly White, but also included Dominicans, Puerto Ricans, and kids from every borough, each carrying different perspectives.

So I learned to flow.

I learned to dap up my boys in the neighborhood, then turn around and discuss philosophy, literature, and politics in a school uniform.

I understood the streets and the scholars.

I could thrive at a block party and in a boardroom.

And here's the key: it was never fake. It was all me.

Code-Switching Is Not Losing Yourself

Too often, people confuse flexibility with fakeness. But the truth is: you are more flexible, dynamic, and multilayered than you realize.

When a good leader steps into a new environment, they don't change their essence—they adjust their expression.

Leadership is knowing how to context-shift without identity-shift.

Paul said it this way: *"I have become all things to all people, so that by all possible means I might save some."* (1 Corinthians 9:22, NIV)

Paul didn't say he lost himself to fit in. He said he spoke people's language so the message could connect.

That's leadership. Not just having a voice—but knowing which voice to use when it matters.

Great Leaders Connect Across Cultures

The best leaders aren't confined to one circle. They move freely among diverse spaces because their calling is bigger than their comfort.

They understand that:
• Every room doesn't require the same tone.
• Every assignment doesn't require the same method.
• Every audience doesn't respond to the same delivery.

But the message, the integrity, and the identity remain the same.

You don't lose who you are—you discover more of who you are.

Each environment pulled a different strength out of me. And I needed them all to become the leader I am today.

Don't Be Afraid to Stretch

Too many leaders stay locked into what feels familiar.

They only lead people who look like them, talk like them, vote like them, or think like them.

But greatness requires stretch.

If your leadership only works in one environment, it's limited. True influence isn't proven in comfort—it's revealed in unfamiliar rooms.

So stretch.

Go to the networking event where you feel like the "only."

Sit at the table where the slang is different, the music is foreign, or the conversation feels over your head.

You belong there too.

Leadership Lessons

• **Code-switching is a skill, not a betrayal.** Use it wisely.

• **Your adaptability is a strength, not a mask.**

• **God doesn't just want to use you in your comfort zone—He wants to use you in your capacity zone.**

The voice you use at work, at home, in the pulpit, or on the block —those are all valid expressions of who you are. You don't have to choose between them. You just have to master them.

Because when God sends you into rooms that don't look like where you came from, it's not so you can become *less* of who you are—

It's so you can become *all* you were born to be.

Check the Weight You're Putting on People

Don't Overburden the Faithful

"If you're not careful, your most loyal people will become your most burdened ones."

Every team has them—the go-to people.

The consistent.

The dependable.

The faithful.

They're the ones who don't need follow-up because they get it done. The ones who show up early, stay late, and rarely complain.

These are your MVPs. Your anchors. Your leadership lifelines.

And because they're solid, the temptation is to keep piling on responsibility. They can handle it, right? They always do.

But here's the hard truth: just because they can carry it doesn't mean they should. And just because they won't say anything doesn't mean they aren't getting tired.

I've Seen It Firsthand

I've seen this a lot in both ministry and the entertainment world.

When leaders discover their MVPs, it's so easy to keep dumping assignments and responsibilities on them. They're proven. They're dependable. And, most importantly, you trust them.

But here's the danger: even the strongest shoulders can only carry so much. I've watched people crash once the weight increased beyond their limits.

It's happened to me. I was doing too much. Instead of trusting others and taking the time to build new talent, I just kept loading up what I could carry. But the work reflected it. Balls were dropped. Excellence slipped. My top soldiers were worn down, and the emerging ones never got developed.

That's when I learned—great leaders don't just lean on the proven. Great leaders spot raw talent and take the time to develop it.

Don't Reward Faithfulness with Overload

In leadership, we often default to the dependable. When something needs to be done, we give it to the one who always delivers.

It feels efficient in the short term—but over time, it becomes toxic. Not because the person isn't gifted, but because they're overloaded.

If you're not careful, you'll start "rewarding" loyalty with more pressure, more responsibility, and more late-night texts—while newer or less consistent team members remain under-challenged and overlooked.

This is how burnout happens—not from laziness, but from overuse.

And this is how resentment grows in the hearts of the loyal.

The Cost of Taking People for Granted

Overburdening the faithful carries long-term consequences:

• They start to feel invisible—valued for what they do, not who they are.

• Their joy turns into duty.

- Their sense of calling becomes a chore.
- Their "yes" becomes heavy, not holy.

You don't just risk burnout—you risk losing their heart for the vision.

And often, by the time you notice they're tired, it's too late. They've either mentally checked out or quietly stepped back. The strongest servant doesn't always storm out—they simply shrink back. And everyone wonders where the fire went.

Moses & Jethro's Warning

In Exodus 18, Moses tried to carry the entire nation on his shoulders. People lined up from morning to night, waiting for him to decide every matter.

Jethro, his father-in-law, saw what was happening and told him plainly:

"What you are doing is not good... You will wear yourself out and the people with you." (Exodus 18:17–18, NIV)

Notice that—Moses would burn out, and so would the people.

Jethro's solution? Delegate. Empower others. Build layers of leadership.

Moses had to release control in order to multiply impact—and protect the very people carrying the weight.

You Have to Develop New Talent

It takes more time and energy to train someone than to hand the task to your veterans. But long-term health requires investment in development.

You can't just lean on the mature—you must make space for the emerging.

- Be patient with the learning curve.
- Resist the urge to "just give it to someone who can do it quicker."

• Value potential, not just perfection.

No strong leader stands alone. Each one was once the risk of another's faith.

David didn't look like a king when Samuel anointed him.

Timothy didn't look like a Paul when Paul first called him "son."

But someone invested, and they grew.

Practical Questions for Leaders

1 Who am I always depending on?

2 Have I asked them how they're doing—not just what they're doing?

3 Am I rewarding loyalty with responsibility or with relief?

4 Am I developing new people, or just defaulting to the veterans?

5 Have I created a culture where rest is as honorable as results?

Build Healthy, Not Just Fast

Leadership isn't just about building great teams—it's about sustaining them.

Your most dependable people deserve more than just a bigger load. They deserve rest. Recognition. Room to breathe. Space to be human.

They shouldn't have to burn out just to keep the system running.

So check the weight. Redistribute the load. Invest in new leaders. Protect the hearts of those who helped you build.

Because the goal isn't just to grow fast—it's to grow healthy.

A fast-growing team can collapse under neglect.

But a healthy team will stand the test of time.

Make It Happen, Money

Leadership Isn't About Knowing Everything—It's About Figuring It Out

Leadership isn't just about having answers—it's about refusing to stop until you find them.

The truth is, leaders are not expected to know everything up front. But they are expected to figure it out.

When plans fall through, when things don't go as expected, when no one else knows what to do—a real leader doesn't freeze. They move into action. They assess. They adjust. They press forward. Even if they have to learn while doing, they figure it out.

Leadership doesn't require perfection—it demands persistence.

Don't Stop at the Question

Most people stop at the question:

- "How are we going to make this work?"
- "What if it fails?"
- "What if we don't have enough?"

Leaders ask the same questions—but they don't camp there. They move past the question and into the solution.

When others are discouraged by obstacles, leaders get curious about the opportunity hidden inside them.

The difference between leaders and spectators? Leaders don't wait for things to be figured out. They go figure it out.

As an Intern at Bad Boy Entertainment

As an intern for P. Diddy at Bad Boy Entertainment, every day felt like a new adventure. No day was the same.

One morning I might be in the office directing calls from five different phone lines—each with its own greeting. If a new album was about to drop, the script was even longer: *"Faith Evans' album Keep the Faith in stores in 3 days. Thank you for calling Bad Boy Entertainment. How can I help you?"*

Another day, I was taking Diddy's son trick-or-treating. The next, I was categorizing a celebrity checklist for an upcoming party, delivering personal invites, picking up individually prepared dinners for a high-stakes meeting, or hunting down a specific Gucci collar for the dog.

The rule was simple: no excuses—make it happen. Even if you had to cross town in 10 minutes during rush hour. Even if the restaurant was closed. Even if the store didn't carry the item. You dared not come back to the office empty-handed.

Think *The Devil Wears Prada*. That was our culture. We prided ourselves on never taking no for an answer and always finding a way.

That mindset—*"Make it happen, money"*—became the unspoken standard. And it shaped me more than I realized.

What I Learned at Bad Boy Entertainment

One of the most impactful lessons I learned early in my career came out of those moments. The pace was relentless. Expectations were sky high. And if you came to your boss with just a problem, you'd get a quick, unapologetic response:

"Figure it out, money!"

That wasn't just a catchphrase—it was a mindset. No one wanted excuses. They wanted to see initiative.

I realized quickly that in high-impact environments, initiative is currency. You didn't earn your place by being problem-free. You earned it by being solution-driven.

That principle has stuck with me ever since—and it applies everywhere, from the boardroom to the church. People don't need leaders who only point out problems. They need leaders who pursue answers until something shifts.

A Personal Example: My Wife's Relentless Pursuit

One of my favorite traits about my wife is her refusal to stop at confusion. She won't rest until she figures it out.

Whether it's technical, logistical, or emotional—she becomes a student of the problem and refuses to be outworked.

She doesn't just pause at the question—she digs, studies, experiments, asks, and pushes. And in the process of solving one issue, she often uncovers five new insights she didn't know she needed.

That's leadership. That's curiosity. That's relentless pursuit. And it's the same mindset every great leader must develop.

Every Problem Has a Solution—If You Stay With It

Some solutions don't show up right away. It may take trial and error. It may include wrong turns and failed attempts. But real leaders don't quit.

They treat failure as feedback.

Closed doors become redirection.

Missteps become material for the next breakthrough.

Thomas Edison famously said: *"I have not failed. I've just found 10,000 ways that won't work."*

That is the essence of leadership—you keep showing up until the solution emerges.

You don't need flawless execution. You need fearless determination.

The "Figure-It-Out" Mindset

Leaders who thrive in challenge:

• Stay solution-minded. They don't waste energy on complaints.

• Take ownership. They don't pass the blame.

• Think creatively. They don't let tradition box them in.

• Ask for help. They build strong circles of wisdom.

• Stay flexible. If Plan A fails, they roll out Plan B.

Leadership isn't about avoiding problems—it's about confronting them and converting them into progress.

You May Not Know Everything—But You Will Figure It Out

Don't let the unknown intimidate you. Every great leader has felt unqualified. Every great solution started as confusion.

The mark of a leader isn't that they know it all—it's that they believe there's always a way forward.

You may feel underprepared or under supported—but if God called you to it, He'll equip you for it.

The same God who gave Noah the blueprint for the ark and Moses the staff for miracles is the same God who will give you the wisdom and strength to figure out your assignment.

So keep going. Keep learning. Keep moving.

You'll figure it out.

Execution Over Intention

Leaders Execute

Everyone has ideas.

Everyone has dreams, plans, concepts, and passions.

But not everyone executes.

Not everyone turns vision into strategy.

Not everyone moves from inspiration to implementation.

That's the difference between a dreamer and a leader. Leaders execute.

Good Intentions Don't Build Anything

Ideas are exciting. They stir the heart and make us feel alive.

But intention without action is just imagination.

Intentions don't raise buildings.

Intentions don't fund missions.

Intentions don't launch ministries.

Intentions don't change lives.

"Do not merely listen to the word, and so deceive yourselves. Do what it says." —James 1:22

God doesn't just bless the idea of obedience—He blesses the execution of it.

Great Ideas Are Everywhere—Executors Are Rare

You're not the only one with a great idea.

You're not the only one who heard from God.

You're not the only one who wants to write a book, start a business, build a team, or launch a movement.

The real question is: Can you execute?

• Can you wake up early, stay late, and put structure behind your strategy?

• Can you lead when motivation wears off?

• Can you manage the mundane steps required to make a vision come alive?

Because ideas don't set you apart—execution does.

A Tool I've Learned: Action Assignments

Over time, I've developed a simple tool for discerning who to truly invest in—whether with time, mentorship, finances, or opportunities. When people come to me with an idea, I give them an action plan.

• You want help with your business? Write a business plan.

• You want help launching a ministry? Write the vision.

• You want help budgeting? List out your actual expenses.

I hear their request, then give them a tangible assignment to complete and bring back. Most of the time, they never return. And that's when I realize: they didn't really want to execute. They only wanted to dream out loud.

I know this because I used to be the same way. For years, I had dozens of ideas for books, scripts, and businesses—but they all stayed in my head. I missed countless opportunities simply because I didn't put pen to paper.

One example still stings. Over 15 years ago, I wrote a play with a friend. I always envisioned turning it into a script, but I never finished it. Then, on a flight, God gave me the opportunity to sit next to a Hollywood producer—for five hours. I pitched him the idea. He loved it. But when I said I didn't have a script yet, his answer was simple: *"Come back when you do."*

What a missed opportunity.

But here's the grace of God: when I finally got serious, did the work, and finished the script, that same producer reconnected with me—and now the project is being negotiated.

That moment shifted me. I stopped parking at ideas. Now, I drive them to execution.

Vision Without Movement Is Delusion

Many people confuse momentum with movement. They think because they're talking, planning, and dreaming, they're building.

But motion without progress is just running in place.

"The plans of the diligent lead surely to abundance, but everyone who is hasty comes only to poverty." — Proverbs 21:5

It's not enough to have a plan—it must be backed by diligence, consistency, and action.

Some people say they're "waiting on God." But often, God is waiting on them.

Waiting becomes disobedience when it becomes an excuse for inaction.

Execution Is What Separates Leaders from Talkers

Leaders...

- Write it down.
- Break it into steps.
- Delegate what they can't do.
- Show up when it's hard.

- Make room for excellence.
- Push through discomfort.
- Refuse to just be inspired—they build.

Execution is where faith and discipline meet.

Jesus Executed the Mission

Jesus didn't just come with a good idea to save the world—He executed the plan of redemption.

He fulfilled prophecy. He walked out purpose. He endured pain. He finished what He started.

"I have glorified You on earth, having accomplished the work that You gave Me to do." — John 17:4

And on the cross, His final words were: *"It is finished."* — John 19:30

Jesus was the ultimate finisher. And as leaders who reflect Him, we must finish too.

You Don't Need a New Word—You Need Follow-Through

Some leaders are addicted to revelation but allergic to responsibility.

They want another prophetic word but haven't obeyed the last one.

They want to start something new when they haven't finished what's already in their hands.

Leadership isn't always about starting—it's about sticking. About finishing. About following through when the excitement is gone.

Execution is often unglamorous—but it's always powerful.

Practical Examples of Execution

• Noah didn't just dream about an ark—he measured wood, cut planks, and built one.

• Nehemiah didn't just grieve about Jerusalem's walls—he organized workers, carried bricks, and rebuilt them.

• Paul didn't just preach visions—he planted churches, wrote letters, and raised leaders.

Dreamers talk about what could happen. Leaders do the work to make it happen.

Final Thought: Don't Just Dream It—Deliver It

You weren't called just to carry vision—you were called to birth it.

And that takes:

• Strategy

• Sacrifice

• Patience

• Consistency

• A refusal to stop until the assignment is fulfilled

The world doesn't need more dreamers. It needs more doers.

Because at the end of the day, history doesn't remember good intentions. It remembers what got finished.

Know Your Yes—Define Your No

Decide Before the Door Opens

If you walk into a room unsure of what you want, don't be surprised if you walk out with less than what you deserve.

In leadership, business, ministry, and life—clarity is currency.

And one of the most underestimated tools a leader can carry is a pre-decided outcome.

Whether it's a negotiation, a meeting, a transition, or a life-altering decision, you must ask yourself in advance:

- What's the goal?
- What am I willing to accept?
- What am I unwilling to compromise?

Without those answers, you're not weak—you're just unprepared.

A Real Moment: The Day Hype Called

I learned this lesson the hard way.

During my senior year of college, I was working as one of the assistants (not even the main one) for the most influential video director I'd ever seen—Hype Williams. He was already a legend. He had just done the film *Belly* and had aspirations for more in the movie space. For me, it was the opportunity of a lifetime. I was young, hungry, and ready to do whatever it took.

One day, he casually asked me to think about becoming his film assistant in Los Angeles.

In my mind, there wasn't anything to think about. It was a definite yes.

Soon after, he invited me to a commercial shoot in L.A.—a Reebok project with rapper Scarface and NBA player Steve Francis. It was my second time in L.A., but this trip was different. We ate at Mr. Chow, stayed in Beverly Hills, and soaked up a little luxury. The sun, the energy, the vibe—I was sold.

A few days later, back in New York, Hype called.

"What did you think of L.A.?" he asked.

I went on and on, bragging about how much I loved it.

"Good," he said. "I want you to move there in five days."

Whoa. I thought this would happen eventually—not immediately. But I didn't hesitate. I said, "Sure."

Then came the real test:

"How much would you need to make the move?"

Without thinking, calculating, or even praying... I blurted out: "$1,000."

"Cool. No problem." Click. Conversation over.

But here's what hit me later: if I had taken even 10 minutes to calculate what I actually needed—to relocate across the country, cover deposits, rent, transportation, and basic needs—I would've asked for far more. Not from greed, but from wisdom.

That moment taught me a priceless truth: lack of preparation always costs you.

Preparation Protects You

If you don't know your number, someone else will define it for you.

If you don't know your boundaries, someone else will push past them.

If you don't know your desired outcome, you become vulnerable to urgency and pressure.

Hype wasn't trying to shortchange me. I shortchanged myself—because I wasn't clear.

And we do this all the time:

• Taking jobs without clarity on growth or pay structure.

• Accepting ministry roles without assessing what we can actually commit to.

• Saying yes to assignments that drain us because we never measured our capacity.

• Walking into negotiations without a "walk away" number—and ending up with terms that betray our value.

Lack of preparation leads to poor negotiation.

Clarity Is a Form of Honor

When you walk into a room prepared, it's not arrogance—it's honor.

You're honoring the opportunity. You're honoring the other person's time. And you're honoring your own worth.

Jesus taught this principle too:

"Suppose one of you wants to build a tower. Won't you first sit down and estimate the cost...?" (Luke 14:28, NIV)

Even heaven requires calculation.

Faith is not foolishness.

Spirituality is not sloppiness.

Preparation is kingdom stewardship.

Know Before You Go

Never walk into a negotiation, meeting, or new opportunity without these three things:

1 Your Desired Outcome – What do I want to walk away with?

2 Your Bottom Line – What's the lowest I'm willing to accept?

3 Your Red Lines – What's non-negotiable to my peace, purpose, or integrity?

If you know these three things, you won't be manipulated by flattery, pressure, or urgency. You can honor the moment without losing yourself in it.

God Is Not Intimidated By Preparation

Sometimes we think asking, planning, or negotiating is unspiritual. But the same God who told Noah the exact dimensions of the ark... the God who gave Moses a detailed blueprint for the tabernacle... the God who gave Joseph the plan to survive famine...

That same God expects us to walk in wisdom.

Don't just show up.

Show up with strategy.

Leadership that Connects
the Dots

Know Enough to Lead Well

"Know well the condition of your flocks, and give attention to your herds..." — Proverbs 27:23 (ESV)

Great leaders don't have to know how to do everything—but they do need to know enough.

One of the most underrated traits of successful leadership is having a general understanding of every area you oversee. Not so you can do every task, but so you can lead every person with clarity, credibility, and care.

Learning by Serving

When I joined Ramp Church, I didn't realize that serving in nearly every ministry—ushers, parking lot, diaconate, music, media, drama, administration, armor bearers, youth ministry, men's ministry, and more—was preparing me for pastoral leadership.

At the time, I was simply being faithful. But those experiences became the foundation for how I now lead those same departments.

God was training my eyes to see every part of the body, not just the platform.

Today, I don't have to be the most skilled musician or the best media tech. I've got people more talented than me in those lanes. But I know enough to:

- Understand their pressures
- Respect their process
- Speak their language
- Make informed decisions that support the whole ministry

You Can't Empower What You Don't Understand

You can't truly empower people if you have no clue what they actually do. That's how unrealistic expectations and disconnected leadership are formed.

When you take time to learn the basics, you lead with:
- **Empathy instead of ego**
- **Insight instead of assumption**
- **Collaboration instead of control**

You don't need to master the lane—but you do need to know the road.

The Corporate Model: What Diddy Taught Me

This principle isn't just for ministry—it runs deep in the business world too.

When I worked for P. Diddy, I saw it in full effect. He wasn't the best producer. He wasn't the most technical artist, marketer, or designer. But here's what made him exceptional:

- He had vision.
- He knew what good looked like.
- He had a gift for identifying and empowering the right people to execute.

From Bad Boy Records to Sean John, from Cîroc to Revolt, his empire wasn't built by doing it all himself—but by adding his instinct, excellence, and direction to teams of experts who brought his vision to life.

He didn't micromanage—he multiplied.

The takeaway? You don't have to do everything. You just need to know enough to recognize who can.

Biblical Examples of Strategic Understanding

• **Moses** wasn't a military commander, yet he understood enough to appoint Joshua and structure tribes for battle.

• **Solomon** didn't build the temple with his own hands, but he knew how to manage craftsmen, architects, and resources.

• **Nehemiah** wasn't a bricklayer, but he understood enough to rally builders, organize shifts, and inspire people to rebuild walls in 52 days.

They weren't experts in every skill—they were leaders who saw the whole and empowered the parts.

Empowerment + Understanding = Scalable Leadership

Knowing a little about a lot allows you to:
• Ask the right questions
• Make smart hires
• Protect your team from burnout
• Champion departments that are often overlooked
• Build unity between departments instead of silos

When you empower others with your trust and understanding, you're not just leading tasks—you're releasing leaders.

Serving gave me insight. Insight gave me trust. Trust gave me influence.

. . .

Leadership Insights: From the Back Lot to the Boardroom

In production, no video shoot works without lighting, sound, cameras, direction, and talent all functioning as one. The best directors don't do it all—but they understand enough to see the big picture and trust the right people.

In ministry, effective pastors know what it takes to make a service run. They appreciate what ushers, parking attendants, youth workers, and volunteers do—and they empower them with freedom and guidance.

In business, the best CEOs can walk into any department—finance, marketing, design, or HR—and hold meaningful conversations. Not because they're experts, but because they respect the expertise of others.

You don't have to be the expert. Just be the leader who sees, respects, and releases.

Because the true power of leadership isn't found in doing everything—it's in knowing enough to connect the pieces, care for the people, and create an environment where everyone can thrive.

Systems Exposes Motives

Structure Reveals

Every leader eventually learns: people don't always show you who they are upfront.

Some come with pure hearts and servant hands.

Others come cloaked in ambition.

But nothing separates the two like structure.

When you start implementing systems—defining roles, setting boundaries, and creating accountability—it doesn't just organize your vision. It reveals hidden agendas.

Structure doesn't just streamline operations. It stirs up spirits.

- The submitted will thrive in it.
- The rebellious will resist it.

If you want to discern alignment, don't just watch who shows up—watch who stays when order is enforced.

Great Vision Attracts Both Partners and Predators

Every divine assignment is magnetic. When God gives you something to build—a church, a business, a movement—it draws people.

Some come because they truly see the vision.

Others come for what the vision might give them.

Great callings attract great people—but they also attract opposition.

• Just like Nehemiah drew builders and enemies.

• Just like Jesus drew disciples and Judas.

You will draw armor bearers and opportunists.

They may say the right things. They may even serve beside you. But structure will expose what charisma can hide.

Structure Exposes What Chaos Conceals

Disorder creates shadows. It gives space for manipulation, hidden motives, and backdoor influence.

But when structure is introduced—when flow is established, expectations are clarified, and boundaries are drawn—people are forced to choose: alignment or exposure.

• Disorganized environments let rebellion breathe.

• Structured environments demand submission—or exit.

That's why some people thrive in chaos: it gives them influence without responsibility, platform without accountability.

But when you install order, those same people often feel threatened—not because you hurt them, but because they were never truly submitted.

God Always Builds With Structure

Structure isn't man-made—it's heaven-born.

• God gave Moses specific instructions for the tabernacle.

• God gave Noah exact dimensions for the ark.

• Paul taught the church to operate in order—spiritually and administratively.

When Moses went up the mountain for divine instructions, the people below made a golden calf. Why?

Because the rebellious prefer inspiration without instruction, and freedom without form.

God's order is not the enemy of His presence—it's the container for it.

Form Doesn't Kill Fire—It Carries It

We often hear, *"Let the Spirit move,"* as if structure stifles the supernatural.

But the early church didn't just operate in fire—they thrived because of form.

• Apostles led.

• Deacons served.

• Communities gave, shared, and grew—in order.

Even Jesus, full of divine power, honored divine process.

• He waited for the right time.

• He submitted to the Father's will.

• He moved within structure—even when He had the authority to override it.

Why? Because spiritual power flows best through submitted vessels.

Rebellious Spirits Resist Accountability

Rebellion doesn't always shout. Sometimes it smiles.

Like Saul, some crave the crown without enduring the process. They want results without relationship, spotlight without submission.

But David shows us another way: even when he had the opportunity to take the throne by force, he honored God's structure and timing.

That's the mark of a true leader: not just charisma, but character under authority.

. . .

Build It Anyway

So build the system.

- Appoint leaders.
- Clarify expectations.
- Define responsibilities.
- Enforce accountability.

And when pushback comes—because it will—remember:
Structure doesn't kill vision. It protects it.

Structure removes confusion, honors God, and provides a foundation for sustained growth.

Build the system—and watch what spirits rise.

Because structure will always expose rebellion. But more importantly, it will empower the right people, elevate the right culture, and secure a legacy that outlives you.

At the end of the day, structure is not about control—it's about clarity. It doesn't exist to make things harder; it exists to make purpose clearer.

The same God who created galaxies also set boundaries for the seas.

The same Spirit who fell at Pentecost also instructed the apostles to *"choose seven men"* to serve tables.

When you resist structure, you're not just resisting man's system—you may be resisting God's order.

But when you embrace it, you align with the way Heaven builds.

So don't fear the tension structure creates—it's just revealing what was already there.

Lean into it. Trust God's design. And watch how order becomes the pathway to overflow.

Let's Play Make Believe

Storytelling Is a Leadership Superpower

Leaders don't just share facts. They frame reality in a way that invites people to believe, to build, and to belong.

Think about it:

• Moses didn't just lead Israel out of Egypt—he gave them a story of covenant and freedom.

• Dr. King didn't just march—he declared, *"I have a dream."*

• Jesus didn't just preach sermons—He told parables that still speak today.

"Where there is no vision, the people perish." — Proverbs 29:18

But vision isn't just something you *have*—it's something you *communicate*. And storytelling is how vision gains feet.

It Starts in the Imagination

The gift of storytelling often begins in childhood:

• Imagining new worlds

• Acting out scenes with toys

• Giving voice to dreams you didn't even know were "dreams" yet

Those childhood stories were early signs that you were called to shape minds, move hearts, and build futures.

You weren't just being dramatic—you were rehearsing leadership.

You weren't just being "extra"—you were learning how to speak the unseen into existence.

"In the beginning, God said..." Creation itself began with a story. And so did your calling.

Great leaders don't just organize people—they orient them toward a bigger narrative. That's why revolutions, revivals, and reformations are always carried on the wings of story.

The Story Must Be Shared to Have Power

A dream that stays in your head won't change anyone.

A vision that lives in silence will die in darkness.

That's why leaders must master the art of sharing their stories:
• Not just the polished parts—but the process
• Not just the *what*—but the *why*
• Not just the blueprint—but the burden
When you tell your story well:
• People don't just follow—they feel
• They don't just work—they believe
• They don't just show up—they carry the vision too
Every great movement was powered by story.

The Civil Rights Movement wasn't just policy—it was the story of dignity, freedom, and justice.

The Gospel itself isn't just doctrine—it is the story of redemption, resurrection, and reconciliation.

Three Marks of a Leader Who Tells the Story
1 They Dream Out Loud
They don't just daydream—they declare. They invite others into

what they see, even before it manifests: *"This is what I see. This is what I believe. This is where we're going."*

2 They Speak with Clarity and Passion

The best stories aren't always long—they're clear, bold, and full of heart. Passion is contagious. People may not remember every detail, but they'll remember how you made them feel.

3 They Connect Emotion to Action

People follow leaders who move both their hearts and their hands. Storytelling ignites something internal that produces external change.

Why Storytelling Matters More Than Ever

We live in an age of noise—tweets, posts, reels, endless content. But people don't remember noise; they remember narratives.

A good story cuts through distraction and lodges in the heart.

• Businesses that tell stories build loyal customers, not just buyers.

• Churches that tell stories build disciples, not just attendees.

• Leaders who tell stories build movements, not just moments.

That's why Jesus' parables are still repeated 2,000 years later. The Good Samaritan still convicts. The Prodigal Son still restores. The Mustard Seed still sparks faith.

Truth wrapped in story has eternal staying power.

Don't Just Dream It—Tell It

You don't need to be a novelist. You don't need to be a preacher.

But if you're a leader—you must be a storyteller. Because your dream will stay invisible until your voice brings it to life.

So speak it. Share it. Shape the world with it.

Because somewhere, someone is waiting to follow a story they can believe in.

And that story... just might be yours.

Your Greatest Asset

People Are the Greatest Asset

If you ask most seasoned leaders what the greatest asset of any organization is, you'll likely hear the same answer: the people.

Not the budget. Not the building. Not the branding.

Your people are the key to everything.

And yet, too many leaders forget this. They push for growth without building people. They chase results while exhausting their team. They focus on the product but neglect the producers.

The truth is this: people are not just a means to an end—they are the mission. How you treat them will either multiply your vision or slowly drain it.

A great leader honors their people. They treat them well, cover them, build them, challenge them, pour into them, and celebrate them. Why? Because they understand something crucial:

If you don't take care of your greatest assets, they can become your greatest liabilities.

. . .

Assets Can Become Liabilities

Take a house, for example. A home is one of the most valuable investments many people will ever make. But if you don't maintain it —if you ignore roof leaks, fail to service the HVAC, or let mold spread in the basement—what was once a blessing becomes a burden.

The value drops.

The repairs multiply.

The cost of neglect increases.

The same principle applies in leadership.

When you neglect your team—when you fail to honor, invest in, and support the very people who carry your vision—you create the conditions for burnout, bitterness, and breakdown.

• Once-committed people become disengaged.

• Loyal followers become silent complainers.

• Talented leaders lose their edge—and eventually, their desire to stay.

But when you care for your people—when you see them not just as tools but as treasures—you create fire. Passion rises. Loyalty deepens. People don't just work with you—they run with you.

Jeff Hoffman's People-First Leadership

The great entrepreneur Jeff Hoffman once made a bold statement: *"My employees never quit."* He attributed this not to salary or perks, but to a simple principle—he helped his people achieve their dreams.

Hoffman asked every employee what their goals in life were, and then wrote those goals on a wall in his office. One wanted to buy a home for his wife. Another wanted to work for an international company. Hoffman didn't just nod—he actively invested in helping them achieve those goals.

His insight was clear: if you invest in your people, they'll invest in you. Their loyalty wasn't bought—it was built. And because their dreams mattered, his vision thrived.

. . .

Personal Lessons

I'll never forget when my boss, Norma Augenblick, surprised me with Broadway tickets to see *Rent* for my birthday—because she knew I aspired to be an actor. That simple gesture added fuel to my fire. I already loved what I did, but that made me want to give even more.

Or the time Sean "P. Diddy" Combs threw a Christmas party and called my name, handing me a bonus in front of the whole staff. That moment of recognition still lives in me.

Or when Hype Williams, known for excellence and creativity, took the staff to the Dominican Republic—not for work, but simply to rest and enjoy. That wasn't just a trip. It was a message: *you matter*.

And then there's Bishop S.Y. Younger—my pastor and spiritual father—who once took a train from Virginia to New York just to support me when I preached at my mother's church. His presence that night spoke louder than any words ever could.

Each of those moments reminded me of this principle: when leaders value their people, people value the vision.

Of course, I've experienced the opposite too: leaders who talked down to me, leaders who let me take the fall to protect their image, leaders who only saw my hands but never my heart. Those experiences taught me what *not* to do—because dishonor at the top poisons the whole system.

If You Lead, Lead Like This...

• Honor your people publicly. A kind word in front of others can do more than a paycheck.

• Cover your people privately. When mistakes happen, shield them, guide them, teach them. Don't let them bleed for your ego.

• Celebrate your people consistently. Don't wait for birthdays and holidays. Celebrate effort, sacrifice, and excellence often.

• Challenge them lovingly. Don't coddle or tolerate laziness. Stretch them, but do it with grace.

• Invest in them personally. Ask about their dreams. Provide opportunities to grow. Pour into them spiritually and professionally.

Final Thought

You can't build anything sustainable without people. And you can't build people if you don't value them.

If you want long-term success in ministry, business, or life—treat your team like the treasure they are.

Because while buildings depreciate and platforms fade, people have the power to carry legacy.

The wisest leaders don't just manage people—they multiply them.

Who's Watching Your Back?

Just **Because They're Behind You Doesn't Mean They're Covering You**

One of the most dangerous assumptions a leader can make is believing that everyone who's close is committed.

Proximity does not equal loyalty.

Support in public doesn't always mean safety in private.

Some people are around you because they believe in you. Others are around because you're beneficial to them.

And if you don't learn to discern the difference between loyalty and usefulness, you'll find yourself betrayed, disappointed, and blindsided.

Because not everyone clapping for you is cheering.

And not everyone walking with you is willing to bleed with you.

Loyalty vs. Usefulness

• Loyal people guard your name in rooms you're not in.

Useful people drop your name in rooms they want access to.

• Loyal people tell you the truth when it's uncomfortable.

Useful people flatter you so they can stay in position.

• Loyal people are with you when things shift.

Useful people disappear when the benefits dry up.

It's easy to confuse the two when things are going well. But crisis always reveals character.

Biblical Example: Judas and John

Jesus had twelve disciples—but they were not all the same.

Judas was close—trusted with the money bag, present at miracles, involved in ministry. But his closeness was rooted in opportunity, not covenant.

John, on the other hand, was loyal. He stood at the cross when others ran. He didn't just follow the ministry—he stayed with the man.

Here's the painful truth: Judas will kiss you just before he betrays you.

That's why discernment is not optional for leaders—it's critical.

Everyone Benefits, But Not Everyone Belongs

As a leader, you must understand: some people are in your life...

• To receive a blessing

• To be developed for their next assignment

• To help for a season

• Or to stay for the long haul

Not everyone is meant for your inner circle.

You can love people and still limit their access.

You can honor their contribution without confusing it with covenant.

How to Discern Who's Really Watching Your Back

1 Watch who corrects you in private, not just who praises you in public. True loyalty shows up in honesty.

2 Pay attention to who's still around when there's no spotlight. No platform, no benefits—who's still serving?

3 Test their fruit, not just their familiarity. Longevity doesn't always mean loyalty.

4 Listen to how they talk when you're not in the room. If support disappears in your absence, that's not loyalty—it's performance.

5 Look for people who value the vision, not just the vibe. If they're only attached to the energy, they'll disconnect when pressure comes.

Everyone Around You Isn't For You

I've learned that being valuable to someone's vision doesn't mean they value you as a person.

They may love your skill.

They may love your access.

They may love the doors your name opens.

But when it's time to protect your heart?

When it's time to stand in spiritual warfare?

When it's time to have your back when you're not in the room?

Only the loyal remain.

This is why trust is earned—not granted by availability.

Leadership requires open arms—but it also requires wise filters.

Closing Thought

The higher you go in leadership, the more selective you must become—not out of paranoia, but out of purpose.

You can't afford to confuse loyalty with usefulness.

Because when the real battle shows up—you won't just need people to stand behind you. You'll need people who will cover you, guard you, and fight for you.

So ask yourself: *Who's really watching my back?*

Then ask the deeper question: *Do they love me—or do they just love what being close to me does for them?*

Discernment is not suspicion. Discernment is protection.

Use it.

When the Leader Retreats
The Power of Stillness in Leadership

If the Leader Panics, Everything Unravels

Leadership isn't just about casting vision—it's about creating calm.

It's easy to lead when everything is smooth. But true leadership is revealed when the winds blow, the storm rises, and all eyes turn to you for direction. In those moments, one thing is essential: the leader can't panic.

Panic spreads like a virus—quick, silent, and devastating. It clouds judgment, amplifies fear, and invites confusion. The leader's posture becomes the emotional thermostat for the team.

• If the leader is frantic, the people will be terrified.

• But if the leader is steady—even without all the answers—the people find peace.

Biblical Stillness: Moses at the Red Sea

In Exodus 14, Israel stood trapped—Pharaoh's army behind them, the Red Sea in front. The people unraveled. Death seemed certain. But Moses didn't panic:

"Do not be afraid. Stand firm and you will see the deliverance the Lord will bring you today." — Exodus 14:13 (NIV)

Moses didn't have a blueprint. He had a relationship. And that gave him the confidence to stand still.

His calm wasn't denial—it was trust.

Imagine if Moses had panicked. Over a million people were following him. His stillness steadied a nation.

Modern Application: A Cockpit in Crisis

In aviation, pilots train for a scenario called loss of visibility. When storm, smoke, or fog blinds the cockpit, they don't rely on feelings—they rely on instruments.

Panic in the cockpit is fatal. Passengers may scream, the co-pilot may freeze—but the captain must stay calm, communicate clearly, and trust the system.

Leaders are no different. In seasons of loss of visibility, teams don't need someone who's emotionally erratic—they need someone who won't flinch.

That calmness doesn't come from charisma; it comes from preparation and inner discipline.

Strategic Withdrawal: Learning to Pause

Sometimes, standing still isn't just a moment—it's a strategy.

Early in my career, I was on a high-pressure video set in Atlanta for LL Cool J. It was a Def Jam production under the legendary Hype Williams. One morning, officials walked onto the set demanding permits—which I had nothing to do with. I couldn't reach Hype. The pressure was thick. Everyone was looking at me.

So I bought time. I quietly walked into a side office, crawled under a desk—not in fear, but in wisdom. I needed silence to think.

That moment taught me: sometimes what looks like hiding is

actually preserving. Sometimes retreat is the only way to avoid making a decision you can't undo.

Don't let pressure force you into an emotional or uninformed choice. What you do in haste today could become tomorrow's regret.

Even Jesus practiced strategic withdrawal. Before choosing His disciples, He spent the night in prayer. Before facing the cross, He retreated to Gethsemane. He didn't withdraw after the battle—He withdrew before it, to gain clarity.

In leadership, retreat is not weakness—it's warfare.

Stillness That Stills the People

In Joshua 3, before Israel crossed the Jordan River, the waters were high and the risk was real. But Joshua's calm settled the people. He reminded them of God's promises.

That's what stillness does—it doesn't mean silence. It means assurance. It tells the people: *"I may not know everything, but I know God. And I know we won't fall apart under pressure."*

Four Principles for Leading Without Panic

1 Pause Before You React

Emotional reactions fuel chaos. Breathe. Pray. Discern. Then move.

2 Speak Calmly and Clearly

In crisis, tone matters more than content. Your calm becomes their compass.

3 Anchor in Values and Vision

When you don't know what to do, remind yourself why you're doing it. Purpose will steer you through uncertainty.

4 Trust God Publicly

Declare your faith out loud. Your confidence in God becomes fuel for the people around you.

. . .

Final Thought

The goal isn't to fake confidence—it's to carry conviction.

You may not always be the smartest, fastest, or most experienced, but if you can stay calm in chaos, God can use you to part seas, lead teams, and bring peace in the storm.

Stillness is your strategy. Retreat is your rhythm.

Leadership doesn't always roar—sometimes it whispers, waits, and watches.

Moments Matter

Moments That Matter

There are moments in life that stay with you forever—not because of the lights, the cameras, or the headlines, but because of the people.

I had the privilege of working on Aaliyah's final music video, *Rock the Boat*. It was a beautiful project—dreamy visuals, beach vibes, and that signature smoothness Aaliyah brought to everything she touched.

The production was split between two locations: one day in Miami, and one day in the Bahamas. I worked the Miami shoot and didn't travel to the Bahamas, but I spent the day with many of the team who did. Some of them never made it back.

Aaliyah. Her makeup artist. Her stylist. Members of her crew. People I laughed with. Talked to. Shared space and energy with. Two days later, the plane carrying them crashed shortly after takeoff in the Bahamas—and just like that, they were gone.

It's hard to explain what that kind of proximity to loss does to you. You replay every interaction in your mind, searching for the last words, the last smiles, the last moments shared. And the lesson that lingers is simple but weighty:

Moments matter. People matter. Time matters.

The Weight of People

We spend so much of our lives chasing the next big thing—another title, another platform, another opportunity. But at the end of the day, what really counts is the impression you leave on the people you encounter.

It's not just what you do—it's *how* you do it.

It's who you are while you're doing it.

And sometimes we're so consumed with the work that we forget to enjoy the people we're working with. We treat coworkers, collaborators, and teammates like functional roles instead of human souls. But these people are more than their job description.

They are living souls, created in the image of God.

They carry real battles, real dreams, real stories, and real families waiting for them at home.

They are God's children before they are our colleagues.

Aaliyah wasn't just talented—she was kind. Her spirit was light. Her presence was warm. Everyone I met that day was gracious and full of laughter. I didn't know it would be our only day together, but I'm grateful it was a good one.

Quiet Rules I Carry

That moment etched some quiet rules into my life:

- Enjoy what you do.
- Cherish every moment.
- Take no one for granted.
- Leave a great impression on everyone you meet.

Because you never know who's fighting a silent battle.

You never know if this is someone's last assignment.

You never know if your smile, your kindness, your integrity, or your presence will become the last memory someone carries.

"Teach us to number our days, that we may gain a heart of wisdom." — Psalm 90:12 (NIV)

Wisdom isn't just about smart decisions. It's about living aware—being present, honoring the now.

Legacy in the Little Things

To this day, whenever I hear *Rock the Boat*, it doesn't feel like just a song. It feels like a moment frozen in time—a final gift from an artist and a team who made their mark not only in music history, but in the hearts of those who knew them, even briefly.

And maybe that's what legacy really is.

Not just what you accomplish.

But how you make people feel.

The impression you leave.

The love you sow.

The light you carry.

So make the most of every room you step into.

Show up fully.

Love deeply.

Work with joy.

And when your name is mentioned—whether tomorrow or decades from now—let it be attached to something that mattered.

Reflection Prompt

Who have you been working with, but not really seeing?

Pause today and:

• Ask someone how they're really doing.

• Give a word of encouragement.

• Be intentional about leaving a good impression.
Because people are not just tools for your task.
They are testimonies in progress—just like you.

Speak Through, Not Around

Leadership Principle: Healthy Leadership Flows Through Structure

Healthy leadership flows through structure, not around it. Speaking through your leaders isn't just wise—it's biblical.

In both church and organizational leadership, the way we communicate can either reinforce structure or slowly unravel it. One of the greatest mistakes leaders make is bypassing those they've appointed by going directly to the people under their care.

It may feel quicker or more efficient, but over time it erodes trust, confuses roles, and weakens the integrity of the team.

And in the church, leadership is not just organizational—it's spiritual. God is a God of order (1 Corinthians 14:40), and our leadership should reflect His nature. That means honoring the structure we prayed for, built, and entrusted to others.

Why This Principle Matters
1. It Honors God's Established Order
When Moses became overwhelmed with the weight of leader-

ship, Jethro gave him timeless advice: delegate. Moses appointed leaders over groups of people (Exodus 18:21–26). Ignoring that structure dishonors the system God designed and undermines those we've empowered.

2. It Strengthens and Empowers Leaders

When you go through your leaders—not around them—you affirm their authority and give them confidence to lead. Constantly stepping in sends the opposite message: *"I don't trust you to handle this."*

3. It Protects the Integrity of the Culture

Culture is not what you preach—it's what you permit. If senior leaders bypass others, the whole team will mirror that behavior. Structure reinforces respect, alignment, and accountability.

4. It Preserves Accountability

Leaders are in place to track details, follow up, and ensure execution. When communication flows through them, accountability stays intact—and senior leaders are freed from micromanaging.

5. It Prevents Confusion and Mixed Messages

When multiple voices speak into the same situation, even with good intentions, it creates chaos. Clear lines of communication ensure unity and prevent frustration.

6. It Develops Future Leaders

Leadership is a muscle. If others never carry weight, they'll never grow. Delegating responsibility trains people to problem-solve, lead meetings, and manage conflict. Titles don't make leaders—experience does.

7. It Frees Senior Leaders to Focus on Vision

Micromanagement drains leaders. When you're tangled in day-to-day tasks, you lose energy for vision, strategy, and discernment. Speaking through your leaders allows you to lead from above.

Jesus and Delegated Authority

Even Jesus worked through structure. He trained the Twelve,

empowered the Seventy, and sent them out with authority to heal, teach, and lead.

When the Roman centurion came to Him in Matthew 8, Jesus marveled at his understanding of authority:

"For I too am a man under authority, with soldiers under me..." (Matthew 8:9)

True authority isn't loud—it's aligned.

The business world understands this as well. CEOs don't manage interns. Regional managers don't bypass supervisors to give tasks directly to entry-level staff. Why? Because they know structure protects order:

- Everyone knows their lane
- Everyone carries their weight
- Everyone trusts the system

Bypassing structure—whether in business or ministry—always breeds insecurity, resentment, and dysfunction.

Order Strengthens the House

Leadership isn't just about getting things done—it's about building people.

When we speak through our leaders, we don't just accomplish tasks—we develop leaders, reinforce structure, and protect the culture of the house.

Disorder might move things faster. But order moves things further.

Built for the Moment - The Power of Habits

Crunch Time Reveals Your Habits

I was watching a close NBA game—the Golden State Warriors vs. the Memphis Grizzlies. It was a nail-biter. The lead kept switching, and every possession mattered. But what stood out most wasn't the athleticism or the big shots—it was the final 30 seconds.

Golden State executed with surgical precision. Memphis made critical mistakes—a pass too late, a rushed shot, a missed rotation. Then the commentator said something I'll never forget:

"Crunch time reveals who has developed the right habits."

At the end of the game, there are no more timeouts. The coach can't draw up a perfect play. The crowd is too loud. The moment is too fast. What you've practiced—what you've trained, what you've made a habit—is what shows up. Nothing more, nothing less.

And that's not just true in sports. It's true in leadership, business, ministry, and life.

There will be moments when you don't have time to call a mentor. No chance to pause for a three-hour prayer. No room for a team huddle. You'll have to move. Decide. Respond.

And in that moment, what kicks in isn't inspiration—it's muscle memory.

If you've built strong habits—integrity, discipline, prayer, study, research, excellence—you won't fold under pressure. You'll perform. But if you haven't... the moment will expose you.

Muscle Memory in Ministry

In ministry, the pressure can be overwhelming. A leader falls. A tragedy strikes. The budget dips. Attendance drops. Your energy is low—and decisions still need to be made.

That's when your spiritual habits carry you. If you've prayed when nobody was watching, fasted when nobody asked, and stayed in the Word when nobody applauded—you'll be ready. You'll lead from overflow. Your decisions won't just be intellectual; they'll be Spirit-led because you've built a consistent rhythm with God.

Muscle Memory in the Marketplace

The same is true in business. Deadlines are tight. Clients demand answers now. You won't always get weeks to prepare. Sometimes, you'll be called into the boardroom on the spot.

And here's the truth: you don't rise to the occasion—you fall to the level of your habits.

That's why leaders who consistently:
• Show up early
• Stay organized
• Prepare for meetings
• Study their industry
• Build relationships
• Ask the right questions
• Treat people well
...stand out. Not because they're lucky, but because they're

trained. They've done the internal work when it wasn't glamorous—so when the spotlight hits, they're steady, calm, and ready.

Lessons from Moses

Look at Moses at the Red Sea. Israel is panicking. Pharaoh's army is closing in. Moses tries to calm the people: *"Stand still and see the salvation of the Lord."* But then he cries out to God.

And God's response is striking: *"Why are you crying out to Me? Stretch out your rod."*

In other words: *"Use what I already gave you."*

That rod had already turned into a serpent. It had turned water into blood. It carried divine authority. The Red Sea moment wasn't the time for something new—it was time to activate what had already been placed in his hand.

Here's the principle: When you build the right habits, God can use what's already in your hand.

He can bless what you've prepared. He can accelerate what you've practiced. He can breathe on what you've built. But if you've neglected preparation, you'll find yourself crying for a miracle in a moment that requires muscle memory.

In Business, Ministry, and Life

• Build your spiritual muscle memory through prayer, Word, and worship.

• Build your leadership muscle memory through preparation, discipline, and consistency.

• Build your business muscle memory through systems, learning, and relationships.

Because when the pressure hits, you won't have time to figure it out—you'll default to who you already are.

Crunch time doesn't create you. It reveals you.

The View from the Ground: Why Leaders Must Walk Among the People

Leaders Must Leave the Office

It was a regular day during a break from classes at Fordham University when a friend and I wandered the streets of Midtown Manhattan. Out of nowhere, a stranger handed us tickets to an advance screening of a movie called *Baby Boy*. We had no expectations—just the excitement of something unexpected.

We watched the film and enjoyed it. But the real lesson came after the credits rolled.

The director—none other than the late, great John Singleton—walked out to personally address the audience. He didn't lecture. He didn't just bask in applause. Instead, he opened the floor. He wanted to hear from us—students, fans, strangers. He asked: *What worked? What didn't? How did the story resonate?*

Singleton, already an acclaimed director, didn't hide behind accolades or assume he had gotten it all right. Instead, he listened. He stood among the people the movie was made for and learned from them.

. . .

Leadership Requires Proximity

Great leadership is more than casting vision from a distance. It requires proximity.

Too many leaders sit in conference rooms drafting policies for people they rarely interact with. They design strategies for customers they've never met. They write training manuals for staff they've never shared a meal with. And then they wonder why there's a disconnect.

Leadership is about people. And if you don't understand the people, you can't lead them well.

Jesus, the greatest leader in history, didn't just preach from mountaintops. He walked through towns, stopped at wells, sat in homes, and wept at gravesides. His influence wasn't detached—it was deeply personal.

God Doesn't Lead From a Distance

"The Word became flesh and dwelt among us..." — John 1:14

God could have remained in heaven. He could have sent messages through angels alone. But instead, He became one of us. He walked our roads, ate at our tables, and entered our suffering.

Jesus didn't just teach in synagogues—He touched lepers, dined with sinners, and listened to the overlooked. He was God in the flesh —and a leader in the trenches.

If Jesus saw the value of walking among the people, how much more should we as pastors, executives, entrepreneurs, and servant-leaders?

The Listening Leader

What Singleton did that day wasn't just a creative choice—it was a leadership principle. He stepped into the audience to gain perspective. He didn't assume his view from the director's chair was the only one that mattered.

Leaders in every sphere should do the same:

- **Business leaders:** Spend a day on the floor with your employees.
- **Pastors:** Don't just preach—sit with members, walk the neighborhood, attend youth night.
- **Content creators:** Read the comments. Ask your audience what's landing and what's not.

Feedback is not weakness. Listening is not a threat. It's one of leadership's most powerful tools.

How to Stay Grounded

Here are four ways to remain close to the people you lead:

1. Schedule Informal Time – Not just meetings. Grab coffee. Walk their space. Visit their world.

2. Create Feedback Loops – Encourage honest input: surveys, Q&As, open office hours.

3. Experience Their World – Walk in their shoes. Answer the customer service line. Use your own product.

4. Value the Outliers – Don't just listen to the loudest voices. The overlooked often carry hidden truth.

From the Streets to Strategy

That surprise movie screening was more than a break from campus life—it was a masterclass in leadership. It reminded me that leaders who listen, who stay grounded, and who connect with real people make better decisions and build stronger teams.

Your authority as a leader isn't tied to your title. It's tied to how well you understand the people you serve. And that kind of understanding only comes when you're willing to leave the office, walk the streets, hear the stories, and open your heart—just like Singleton did that day in Manhattan.

Purpose Shouldn't Cost You Your Peace

Loving What You Do Without Losing Yourself

"Loving what you do is a gift—but letting it consume you is a trap."

When you're passionate about your calling, it's hard to turn it off. The mission feels urgent. The vision is exciting. The results weigh on your shoulders. But when you never step away, even something God-given can become toxic.

You can be so consumed by your work that you forget to live. You can be so driven by your assignment that you abandon your relationships. You can be so in love with the grind that you wake up one day exhausted, alone, and burnt out.

Purpose should never cost you your peace. And your calling should never cost you your covenant—with your spouse, your children, your health, or your sanity.

A Personal Story: Missing Christmas for the Grind

I was planning my annual Christmas trip to visit my mom, sisters, and friends back in New York. The office usually shut down in

December, and I'd spend almost two weeks at home. The music video business had been booming all year—we were traveling across the country, money was flowing, and Hype Williams was grooming me to become a producer, which meant bigger checks.

I loved the crew. We were family. I loved meeting artists, working with record label executives, and—if I'm honest—the afterparties too. But I hadn't seen my family all year because of the workload, and they couldn't come visit me either.

Then, just a week before my trip, Hype called me. Def Jam had booked us for five music videos—back-to-back—for Ne-Yo, LL Cool J, Jennifer Lopez, Young Jeezy, and T.I. The shoots would run right through Christmas. He asked, "Are you down?"

I wanted to say, "Do you even have to ask?" Of course I was down. Let's make the money. I figured I'd send my family nice gifts to make up for missing the time. But once the shoots began, something felt different. What normally felt like excitement now felt empty. The sets, the lights, even the money—it didn't feel worth missing home. I realized the grind had pulled me so far in that I was losing touch with what mattered most.

Bishop S.Y. Younger once gave me a sobering perspective. He said, "If you only see your father once a year, and God grants him another ten years of life, you'll only see him ten more times before he goes home." That hit me deeply. It made me think about how fleeting time really is, and how easily we trade what matters most for what matters now.

Work Is a Part of Life—Not All of It

We often say things like "I'm all in" or "I'm married to the game." But when you idolize your work, you devalue everything else.

God didn't design you to be available 24/7 to a job or ministry. He designed you for rhythm: six days of work, one day of rest. Time to build. Time to breathe.

Being driven is not the same as being disciplined. Discipline includes knowing when to:
- Shut the laptop
- Turn off notifications
- Be present at dinner
- Listen to your kids
- Watch a movie with your spouse
- See the doctor
- Sleep

Remember: burnout doesn't start in the body—it starts in the mind. And when your mind never unplugs, eventually your body will.

When the Mission Becomes an Addiction

Work becomes toxic when it:
- Replaces your identity ("Who am I without this?")
- Hijacks your relationships ("They'll understand I'm busy.")
- Dominates your emotions (you're only happy when you're working)
- Becomes your only language (you can't talk about anything else)

Your family doesn't want your leftovers. They want your attention, your laughter, your patience—not just your paychecks or titles.

Even Jesus Withdrew

Jesus was doing the most important work in human history—and He still stepped away:

"But Jesus often withdrew to lonely places and prayed." — Luke 5:16

He didn't heal 24/7. He knew the power of boundaries. He modeled separation so restoration could happen. If He needed space to recharge, so do we.

. . .

Practical Steps to Reclaim Your Life

1. Set Boundaries and Keep Them

If you're answering emails at midnight or taking calls during dinner, you're training people to believe you're always available. Boundaries aren't just for others—they're for you. Protect mornings, evenings, and family time like you would a meeting with your boss.

2. Schedule Joy

Don't just pencil in meetings—pencil in life. Date nights, game nights, workouts, friendships, and hobbies keep your soul alive. Joy isn't fluff—it's fuel.

3. Protect the Sabbath

Whether it's Saturday, Sunday, or Monday—take a real day off. No work. No ministry calls. No guilt. The Sabbath isn't a suggestion; it's a commandment. Rest is worship, not weakness.

4. Talk About More Than Work

If the only stories you share are from the office or pulpit, your world is too small. Engage your family in conversations that aren't tied to deadlines, sermons, or projects.

5. Celebrate Presence, Not Just Productivity

Your worth is not measured by output alone. Put the phone away at your child's recital. Sit at the dinner table without distraction. Laugh without checking notifications. Presence is often the greatest gift you can give.

Closing Thought

You are more than what you do. Your kids need you whole. Your marriage needs your time. Your body needs your attention. Your soul needs your stillness.

The goal isn't just to build a legacy out there. It's to have life and joy in here—at home, with your people, and in your own soul.

Don't wait for a breakdown to find balance. Pursue purpose, but don't abandon peace. The work will always be there. But the people won't.

The Seduction of the Spotlight

Influence, Temptation, and Stewardship

Influence may look glamorous from the outside, but behind the applause and open doors lies a quieter, more dangerous reality: temptation.

The moment you step into visibility, you're not just seen—you're studied, sought after, and sometimes seduced.

This isn't simply about scandal—it's about stewardship. Because what you do with your platform will either protect your purpose or sabotage your future.

Leadership Is Magnetic

When you step into position—carrying purpose, power, or visibility—people are drawn to you. Some are drawn to your calling. Others to your character. But not everyone comes with pure intentions.

- Some are pulled in by your status.
- Others by the rooms you enter.
- Many by the doors they believe you can open.

With influence comes opportunity. But make no mistake—it also brings temptation. It's why so many people are attracted to pastors. The anointing, the power, and the influence is enticing.

The Assignment That Opened My Eyes

Early in my career, I was tasked with casting extras for a music video featuring 50 Cent and The Game for their hit record *How We Do*.

One scene required dozens of women to play club-goers, so I created a simple Craigslist ad: no names, just "major music video featuring platinum-selling artists."

I posted it Friday night. By Saturday morning, I had over 300 responses.

I selected about 100 women for the shoot, but what shocked me were the messages that accompanied the responses. Some included explicit photos. Others made inappropriate offers.

These women didn't know me. Had never seen me. They weren't responding to me—they were responding to access.

It wasn't about who I was. It was about where I stood.

Power attracts. Influence seduces. And if you're not grounded in purpose, you'll fall for what your position invites.

Influence Will Make You a Target

The day of the shoot only confirmed what I had sensed: influence doesn't just attract opportunity—it attracts opposition.

People project onto you their hopes, their agendas, and their temptations. That's why leadership feels heavy—it's not just your assignment you're carrying, but the weight of every eye watching.

• Ask Joseph. His anointing brought him favor—but also Potiphar's wife.

• Ask David. His crown gave him power—but also positioned him for temptation on a rooftop.

• Ask Jesus. His Spirit-led ministry drew crowds—but also drew Satan into the wilderness with offers of shortcuts and compromise.

Leadership makes you magnetic. But magnets don't just attract gold—they also pull in garbage.

The Danger of Unchecked Desire

Here's the sobering truth: the same drive that fuels your ambition can destroy your destiny if it isn't surrendered to God.

"Each one is tempted when he is drawn away by his own desires and enticed." — James 1:14

Temptation doesn't start on the outside—it starts on the inside. The platform doesn't create weakness; it reveals it.

That's why leaders must build guardrails before the spotlight hits.

Leaders Set the Standard—Before the Storm

Integrity isn't improvised in the moment—it's decided in advance.

• Joseph fled before the robe was even in Potiphar's wife's hands.

• Daniel resolved in his heart before he was tested at the king's table.

• Jesus quoted Scripture in the wilderness before Satan could twist it.

Your gifting may open doors, but it's your character that determines if you'll stay in the room.

Guard the Vessel, Protect the Gift

Paul gave this warning:

"I discipline my body and keep it under control, lest after preaching to others I myself should be disqualified." — 1 Corinthians 9:27

The enemy doesn't mind if you preach truth, build teams, or gain influence—if he can get you to disqualify yourself in private.

Guard your vessel. Protect the gift. Don't just build an image—build integrity.

Final Charge: Be Driven, But Be Disciplined

Leadership will always make you a target—not just because of what you carry, but because of what your fall would cost.

The world doesn't need more magnetic personalities. It needs more trustworthy ones.

Be faithful with the spotlight. Steward the platform. Protect your heart.

Because your influence is too valuable to waste on temptation.

And your calling is too great to trade for compromise.

Beyond the Sale — Building Relationships Over Results

People Over Performance

"Let love be genuine. Abhor what is evil; hold fast to what is good. Love one another with brotherly affection. Outdo one another in showing honor." – Romans 12:9–10 (ESV)

It's one thing to be effective. It's another thing to be impactful.

During my time at Enterprise Rent-A-Car, I was excelling. I was a top salesman—closing deals, earning promotions, climbing fast. Within months, I landed at the best branch in New York City—a place reserved for top performers. I had my system. I knew how to close. I could upsell with confidence, and customers responded.

One day, after sealing a solid transaction, a veteran at the branch pulled me aside.

"Great sale," he said with a smile. Then he asked:

"But what did you learn about that person?"

I froze. I had been so focused on getting the sale that I couldn't remember anything about the customer. Not their name. Not their story. Nothing.

He looked me in the eye and said:

"It's great that you got the sale... but it would be better if you built a relationship—so they'd always come back."

That moment forever shifted how I view leadership, sales, and ministry.

People Over Performance

In leadership—especially in ministry—it's easy to get so focused on the win that we forget the who.

But God doesn't just call us to produce; He calls us to connect. He's not just the God of results—He's the God of relationship.

"And this is eternal life, that they know You, the only true God..." – John 17:3 (ESV)

Jesus was intentional with people. Zacchaeus in the tree. The woman at the well. Nicodemus by night. He didn't just perform miracles—He built relationships.

You can impress people with performance, but you impact them with presence.

You're Not Leading Robots—You're Leading Souls

People aren't just assignments—they're souls. And souls don't respond to systems; they respond to sincerity.

When people know you care, they trust you. They follow—not because of your title, but because of your heart.

Metrics matter: numbers, attendance, giving, growth. But real ministry is messy and relational. It requires time, listening, and remembering their name.

"Be devoted to one another in love. Honor one another above yourselves." – Romans 12:10 (NIV)

Legacy Isn't Built on Transactions

Legacy isn't measured by how many people followed your

instructions. It's measured by how many people felt seen, known, and valued under your leadership.

The best leaders aren't always the ones with the biggest stages. Often, they're the ones who pause long enough to ask:

"But how's your heart?"

A sale is good, but trust is better. Trust produces loyalty, and loyalty multiplies impact. A customer may never remember the car I sold them—but they'll remember how I made them feel.

One moment of genuine connection can open the door to a lifetime of influence.

Slow Down and See People

Whether you're leading a team, building a business, or pastoring a congregation—don't be so focused on the goal that you miss the soul.

- Slow down.
- Ask questions.
- Remember birthdays.
- Celebrate wins.
- Mourn losses.

Be a leader people can talk to—not just take orders from.

Practical Application: Building Relational Equity

1. Learn Names & Stories – A remembered name or child's birthday is never small.

2. Check In, Not Just Check Off – Ask how they're doing, not just what they're doing.

3. Value People Beyond Roles – Remind them they matter outside of performance.

4. Listen Without an Agenda – Sometimes people don't need solutions; they need presence.

5. Lead with Honor – Publicly celebrate people for who they are, not just what they do.

Final Thought

Results are good. Systems are necessary. Metrics matter. But they're not the point. People are.

When love, presence, and relationship drive your leadership, results will follow—but more importantly, lives will be changed.

Because at the end of the day, no one remembers how many sales you closed.

They remember how you made them feel.

Leading Difficult People

Leading Difficult People

Every leader—no matter how anointed, skilled, or experienced—will eventually face the challenge of leading difficult people. From rebellious team members to passive-aggressive followers, difficult people are not interruptions to your leadership journey; they are part of your training ground.

Moses knew this well. He led a nation that murmured, doubted him, rebelled, and even built idols. Yet despite their resistance, God still called Moses *"faithful in all My house"* (Numbers 12:7). That's leadership maturity—staying faithful to God and the mission, even when the people you lead make it hard.

A Personal Story: Learning to Lead Through Conflict

When I was directing a school play, I had a crew member who constantly challenged everything I said. It wasn't outright rebellion—it was little things. They'd show up late, cut corners, and then argue whenever I corrected them.

At first, I took it personally. I thought they just didn't respect me.

But after a heated exchange one night during rehearsal, I pulled them aside. Instead of arguing, I asked a simple question: *"What's really going on?"*

That's when it came out. They had been overlooked and mistreated on past productions, never trusted with real responsibility. What I was seeing as rebellion was really insecurity and a fear of being taken advantage of again.

I realized that leading difficult people requires more than reaction—it requires discernment. It wasn't about winning the argument. It was about winning the person. When I shifted from frustration to understanding, things improved. They didn't become perfect overnight, but they became loyal because they finally felt seen.

That experience taught me this: difficult people are often carrying difficult histories. And as leaders, we must learn to lead with both truth and grace.

Understand the Root, Not Just the Behavior

Difficult behavior often masks deeper issues: fear, insecurity, trauma, or pride.

In ministry and in the workplace, a resistant team member may not actually be rebellious—they may be carrying unhealed wounds from past leadership or disappointments.

Lead with discernment, not just reaction. Instead of only addressing surface behavior, ask: *"What's underneath this?"* Sometimes the loudest critic in the room is simply the most insecure voice in the room.

Don't Sacrifice Vision for Approval

Trying to appease difficult people can derail your mission.

Nehemiah faced opposition from Sanballat and Tobiah, but he refused to come down from the wall to entertain distractions (Nehemiah 6:3). He stayed focused on the assignment.

As a leader, your call must be louder than your need to be liked. Leaders who bend too far for approval eventually break the vision.

Correct Without Crushing

Correction is necessary, but how you do it matters.

Go into tough conversations with the goal of reconciliation—even if the outcome is releasing someone. Don't just tear down; aim to rebuild.

"Restore such a one in a spirit of meekness." — Galatians 6:1

Leadership Principle:

• Correction without love feels like rejection.

• Love without correction feels like neglect.

Balance both, and while people may resist you in the moment, they will respect you in the long run.

Set Boundaries, Not Bitterness

You are responsible *to* people, but not *for* them. Boundaries protect your focus, your energy, and your peace.

Even Jesus regularly withdrew from the crowds—and at times even from His disciples—to reset and pray (Luke 5:16).

Access should be earned, not assumed. Boundaries aren't unspiritual; they are essential. Guard your core so you can serve from overflow, not exhaustion.

Recognize When to Release

Not everyone is meant to go with you to the next level.

• Saul's jealousy made him dangerous. David honored him, but never returned to live in his courts.

• Paul and Barnabas had a sharp disagreement that led to a split (Acts 15). Yet both continued in fruitful ministry.

Not every separation is a failure. Some are divine redirections.

Sometimes releasing someone preserves both the mission and their dignity.

Love the Person, Lead the Mission

Even difficult people are God's people. Leadership maturity is proven not in how you treat the cooperative ones, but in how you handle the challenging ones.

Jesus washed Judas' feet, even knowing he would betray Him. He restored Peter, the same man who denied Him three times, and called him a rock of the Church.

Love doesn't excuse dysfunction—but it does refuse to dehumanize.

Difficult People Are Divine Tools

Difficult people are not just obstacles; they are opportunities in disguise. They are sandpaper in God's hand, smoothing out your rough edges.

• Moses' legacy wasn't just shaped at the Red Sea—it was forged in the wilderness with a murmuring people.

• David's character wasn't proven only on the throne—it was refined while navigating Saul's jealousy.

• Jesus' love wasn't just displayed to the crowds—it was tested when He washed Judas' feet.

Difficult people remind us: leadership isn't about ease—it's about endurance. It's not about popularity—it's about perseverance. True leadership isn't measured when everyone applauds—it's measured when someone resists, and you still respond with grace, grit, and growth.

And here's the sobering truth: sometimes the "difficult person" isn't on your team—it's in you. God uses conflict not only to reveal others' weaknesses but also to expose our own.

. . .

Final Thought

Your greatest testimony as a leader won't be how you handled the easy ones—it will be how you shepherded the hard ones.

When you lead with both courage and compassion, you don't just move the vision forward—you mirror the heart of Christ.

So don't run from difficult people. Don't resent them. Let them refine you. See them as God's instruments, shaping you into a wiser, stronger, and more Christlike leader.

Work Smart, not just hard

Working Around the Clock Is Not a Badge of Honor

It's often a badge of inefficiency, poor planning, and lack of strategy.

The grind is glorified in our culture. We post screenshots of 3 a.m. work sessions, wear exhaustion like a medal, and pride ourselves on how little rest we get. But real leadership isn't measured by hours logged—it's measured by impact.

Yes, there will be seasons of sacrifice—late nights, early mornings, deadlines that stretch you. Building anything worthwhile costs something. But if you're always overwhelmed, always behind, always grinding—it's not dedication, it's dysfunction. And leaders who idolize burnout usually burn out the people they lead, too.

Efficiency Is the Edge

Leadership isn't about doing more—it's about doing better. Effective leaders don't just push harder; they think sharper. They build systems, delegate strategically, and prioritize what actually moves the mission forward.

Anybody can hustle all day. But what if you could do in two days what takes others a week? That's not laziness—it's leadership intelligence. That's strategy. And it frees you to dream about what's next while others are still buried in their first draft.

In a culture that equates busyness with success, efficiency becomes your secret weapon.

A Lesson From College: Hustle vs. Strategy

My college years taught me both sides of the grind.

On one hand, I was juggling 20 credits, a job, and an internship. I thought pulling all-nighters made me impressive. I wore exhaustion like a badge of honor. But the truth? I was sloppy, distracted, and forgetful. My work wasn't sharp—it was scattered. I was grinding hard but not producing my best.

Then came my senior year. Dr. Naison assigned us a 100-page paper on the very first day of class, due on the last. Normally, I would have procrastinated and tried to cram it all in during finals week. But something in my spirit told me this wasn't the type of assignment I could push to the end.

So I pulled out my calendar, counted the weeks in the semester, and came up with a plan: ten pages per week. By pacing myself and staying consistent, I finished with time to spare. No frantic late nights. No sloppy last-minute panic. For one of the first times, I worked smart instead of just working hard.

Looking back, I believe God was teaching me a principle: hustle without strategy leads to burnout, but consistency and planning lead to excellence.

Biblical Wisdom: Jesus and the Rhythm of Rest

Even Jesus—God in the flesh—worked with intention. He healed multitudes, preached to crowds, and trained disciples. But He also withdrew to rest and pray.

"Very early in the morning... Jesus got up, left the house and went off to a solitary place, where he prayed." — Mark 1:35

His power didn't come from endless hustle. It came from alignment. From clarity. From time with the Father.

If Jesus didn't grind around the clock to fulfill His mission, why do we think we must?

Why Grinding Isn't Always Glorifying

1. Overwork can glorify self, not God. It puts you at the center instead of pointing to the God who gives grace and strategy.

2. Fatigue kills creativity. Exhaustion may help you finish a task, but rest helps you see the vision.

3. Grind culture creates shallow work. Constant motion doesn't guarantee progress. You can be busy and still go nowhere.

How Leaders Work Smarter

• **Prioritize Impact Over Activity** – Ask: What one thing can I do today that makes everything else easier or unnecessary?

• **Build Better Systems** – Automate what you can. Delegate what you shouldn't be doing. Free yourself to lead.

• **Protect Thinking Time** – Great ideas rarely come when you're buried in tasks. Create space to think.

• **Rest Without Guilt** – Leaders who never rest lead people into unrest. Model sustainability.

• **Audit Your Calendar** – Not everything deserves a yes. Smart leaders cut what doesn't move the mission forward.

Closing Thought

Hard work matters. But wise work multiplies.

Don't grind for the applause of exhaustion. Work for impact. Build with strategy. Let others brag about sleepless nights while you're already moving into your next God-given assignment.

Because when you learn to work smart, you don't just keep up—you rise above.

Uncovered is Unsafe

Every Leader Needs Accountability

There's a dangerous myth in leadership: the higher you go, the less you need covering.

The truth? The higher you go, the more accountability you need. Because when no one is checking you, no one is protecting you.

Unaccountable leaders aren't just a risk to themselves—they're a risk to their teams, their legacy, and the mission. It doesn't matter how gifted, successful, or followed you are—if you don't answer to someone, you're in danger.

Covering Protects, It Doesn't Restrict

From Genesis to Revelation, accountability is a biblical principle:
- Adam was covered by God.
- Eve was given to Adam, yet still accountable to God.
- Moses had Jethro, who taught him to delegate.
- David had Nathan, who confronted him with courage.
- Paul had the Antioch church as a sending team.

• Jesus Himself said, "I do only what the Father tells me" (John 5:19).

Accountability doesn't weaken you—it protects you.

Too many leaders treat submission like demotion. But submission is actually strength under control. It says:

• "I'm gifted, but I'm not rogue."

• "I'm anointed, but I'm not untouchable."

• "I lead others, but I'm not unled."

Covering doesn't cage you—it guards the calling inside you.

The Danger of Living Unchecked

Unchecked leaders always become unsafe leaders.

Without accountability:

• Pride grows unchecked.

• Sin festers in secret.

• Emotions go unmanaged.

• Decisions become reckless.

• People become disposable.

• The leader drifts—often without realizing it.

It starts subtly:

• "I don't need to run this by anyone."

• "They wouldn't understand."

• "God told me, so I don't need to explain."

But slowly, you become the only voice you trust. That's not revelation—it's isolation.

"In the multitude of counselors there is safety." — Proverbs 11:14

Not perfection. Not control. Safety.

Because when you're covered, someone loves you enough to pull your coattail, ask the hard questions, and remind you: the call of God doesn't exempt you from correction—it demands it.

Who Do Leaders Run To?

Here's the reality: leaders may pour into many, but they must also run to someone.

You have to have a person—or better yet, a circle—who can check you, cover you, be raw with you, and offer you a safe place. This person should not be impressed by you or your gift. They shouldn't be intimidated by your influence or blinded by your platform.

You need someone who can look you in the eye and say, "That wasn't wise," or "You're not okay, let's deal with this."

Every leader needs a refuge where they can be honest, vulnerable, and unmasked without fear of judgment or exploitation.

Without that, even the strongest leader will eventually collapse under the pressure of isolation.

Accountability Isn't Just for the Fallen—It's for the Faithful

We often think accountability is damage control after a failure. But healthy accountability isn't about catching you—it's about keeping you.

It's not crisis management. It's destiny maintenance.

Practical rhythms of accountability include:

• Giving trusted voices permission to say no.

• Checking with mentors before major decisions.

• Letting people ask about your spiritual, emotional, and relational health.

• Building consistent spaces for confession and transparency.

Accountability isn't just about morality—it's about longevity. If you want to last, you need guardrails that sustain you.

Who Covers You When You're Covering Others?

Leaders pour out constantly. You make decisions, pray, discern, direct, and cover others.

But here's the hard truth: pourers still need pitchers.

- Who sees you when you're tired?
- Who knows when your heart is off?
- Who checks on your family, your thoughts, your blind spots?

Even the best leaders have limits. Without someone covering you, you'll start leading empty. And leading from emptiness always ends in damage.

Ask yourself:

- Who can rebuke me without me shutting down?
- Who knows the real me, not just the role?
- Who has full access to my process?

Accountability Is Covenant, Not Control

Find people who cover you, not control you.

- Accountability empowers—it doesn't micromanage.
- It protects—it doesn't restrict.
- It grows you—it doesn't shrink you.

There's a difference between being watched and being walked with.

A true covering doesn't just monitor you—they pray for you, fight for you, and help you become who God has called you to be.

At Ramp Church, I've had the gift of being covered by leaders like Bishop S.Y. Younger—leaders who carry the authority to correct, but also the heart to care. That balance has shaped me more than any title ever could.

Be Accountable Before You Become a Cautionary Tale

We've all seen leaders fall. Ministries crumble. Talents wasted. Not because they weren't gifted—but because no one could tell them, "That's not wise."

Let that be a warning—and an invitation.

You don't have to be a cautionary tale. You can be a testimony of integrity. A leader who didn't just start well, but finished strong.

Not because you were perfect. But because you were accountable.

Can It Run Without You?

The True Test of Leadership: What Happens When You're Gone

You don't measure the strength of a leader by what happens when they're in the room.

You measure it by what happens when they're not.

If a business collapses, a ministry flounders, or a team panics the moment the leader takes a day off, goes on vacation, or steps into sabbatical—that's not strength. That's dependency disguised as excellence.

Leadership is not about being the center of everything. It's about building systems, teams, and cultures that thrive—even in your absence.

If Everything Requires You, It's Not Scalable

Good leaders often become bottlenecks without realizing it. Because they know the vision—or how to "do it right"—they insert themselves into every meeting, decision, and detail.

But here's the truth:

- You can't scale what you won't release.
- You can't rest when you won't trust.
- You can't grow when you refuse to delegate.

If everything depends on you, then nothing is truly empowered. Leadership isn't about what you can personally do—it's about what can survive without you.

Jesus Empowered, Then Departed

Jesus modeled this perfectly.

He could have stayed forever—running every revival, teaching every sermon, healing every sick person. But instead, He trained, equipped, and sent disciples.

Even after the resurrection, He didn't linger. He told them:

"It is better for you that I go..." — John 16:7

Why? Because the strength of the mission would be proven in His absence—not His constant presence.

A Ramp Church Example

The culture of Ramp Church International is God-inspired and shaped by Bishop S.Y. Younger, our founder and senior pastor. Bishop is a prayer warrior, a profound teacher, a prophetic voice, a worshipper, a praiser, and above all, a man who genuinely loves people. He has the unique ability to make someone feel like family the very first time they meet him. His DNA is woven throughout Ramp Church—from the way we worship to the way we serve— and God has blessed him with the gift to usher in His presence through song and to shift people to higher levels through preaching.

We often say you have to visit Ramp at least once in your life because the experience is unforgettable. Yet we never take for granted that we get to experience this gift week after week.

But here's the thing: Bishop has always taught us that ministry should never revolve around one man. It should never be personality-driven. And he doesn't just teach it—he lives it.

On Sundays when Bishop is out of town, Ramp doesn't lose its rhythm. Whether it's another pastor, elder, deacon, or even one of the brothers or sisters preaching, God's glory still fills the room. Worship and praise remain alive. People still flood the altar, giving their lives to Christ and being baptized. Even in Bishop's absence, the anointing is evident.

That's the mark of healthy leadership. True leadership builds something that lasts beyond the leader's immediate presence.

Absence Should Reveal Strength—Not Dysfunction

A leader's absence should not reveal chaos. It should reveal competency.

A healthy organization continues with clarity and excellence because the leader has prepared it for moments without them. That means:

- Training others
- Empowering decision-makers
- Establishing systems
- Creating clarity

If your absence exposes disorganization, codependency, or insecurity—it's not a rest problem. It's a reproduction problem.

Sustainability Is a Legacy Decision

Sustainability isn't built for today—it's built for tomorrow.

If everything crumbles when you're away, you haven't built a movement—you've built a moment.

The true legacy of a leader isn't measured by how loudly they were celebrated, but by how strongly their systems endured.

Ask yourself:

- Have I duplicated my thinking in others?

• Have I raised leaders who understand the mission without needing my constant voice?

• Can things move forward if I'm gone for a week, a month, or even a season?

If not, you're not finished building.

Good Leaders Train. Great Leaders Replace Themselves

Don't just empower people to assist you—empower them to own what you once carried.

Let them:

• Run the room

• Make the call

• Cast the vision

• Hold the standard

Not so they can mimic you—but so the mission can mature beyond you.

Sabbatical Shouldn't Mean Sabotage

It's not just about Sunday service running smoothly while the pastor is away. It's about the culture staying strong, the teams staying united, and the mission staying active—because leadership created structure, not spotlight.

Rest should never feel like abandonment. A break shouldn't break the system.

If you're afraid to step away, it's usually because:

1. You've created a culture of dependence, or

2. You've failed to equip replacements.

Neither honors God. Neither builds legacy.

Build What Can Outlive You

You were never called to be the sole engine of the organization—you were called to build it.

• Build teams that lead in your absence.

• Build systems that function without your hand on every wheel.

• Build a culture that doesn't collapse under transition.

• Build a structure that doesn't panic in your pause.

Because if your presence is the only thing holding it together, your absence will be the very thing that tears it apart.